Rebels, Saints, and SINNERS

Rebels, Saints, and Sinners

Savannah's Rich History and Colorful Personalities

By Timothy Daiss

PELICAN PUBLISHING COMPANY
Gretna 2002

*The word "Pelican" and the depiction of a pelican are trademarks
of Pelican Publishing Company, Inc., and are registered
in the U.S. Patent and Trademark Office.*

Library of Congress Cataloging-in-Publication Data

Daiss, Timothy.
  Rebels, saints, and sinners : Savannah's rich history and colorful
personalities / Timothy Daiss.
    p. cm.
  ISBN 1-58980-049-4 (alk. paper)
    1. Savannah (Ga.)—History—Annecdotes. 2. Savannah
(Ga.)—Biography—Anecdotes. I. Title.
  F294.S2 D35 2002
  975'8'724—dc21
                                            2002004289

The article "Edward C. Anderson: Mayor Becomes Arms Dealer,"
pp. 192-196, is reprinted with the permission of *Savannah Magazine*.

Printed in the United States of America
Published by Pelican Publishing Company
1000 Burmaster Street, Gretna, Louisiana 70053

Contents

Preface

The majority of the stories in this book were written for local newspapers and magazines, primarily Morris Multimedia and its subsidiaries.

From the moment I conducted research for the first article, I became enthralled with the project. The opportunity to write about Savannah's history gave me the chance to dig deeply into the city's fabric, both its social and its political institutions. I rubbed shoulders with the former federal judges, ex-cops, attorneys, both the reputable and the not so reputable, as well as the city's social elite, former bookies, and what used to be referred to as gangsters.

Some of the essays in this work tell the story of the founding and settling of Savannah, and subsequently Georgia, one of America's thirteen original colonies. Other stories, however, such as "Getting Away with Murder," "The Day Babe Ruth Played in Savannah," and "Elvis Rocks Savannah," had never been told, at least in print. And it is these stories that I think capture the essence of the city's history, albeit "the good, the bad, and the ugly," to borrow the title of a Clint Eastwood movie.

Hopefully, the broad assortment and range of stories in this work will inform, entertain, and most of all enlighten all who wonder about Savannah and what all the fuss is about.

Rebels, Saints, and SINNERS

PART ONE:
The Events

The Sinking of the *Pulaski*

B uilt by the Savannah and Charleston Steam Packet Company, the steamship *Pulaski* was the pride of both cities. She was a sleek, wooden vessel measuring 206 feet in length with a 25-foot beam, a depth of 13 feet, 7 inches, and displaced 687 tons.

Boasting of the *Pulaski,* an April 1838 advertisement in the *Georgian* proclaimed:

> No expense has been spared to have a vessel to answer the purpose she is intended to accomplish. Her engine—one of the best ever made in this country, of 225 horsepower: her boilers are of the best copper, and great strength. Her qualities as a sea vessel for ease, safety, and speed are superior to any steamer that ever floated on the American waters.

An elaborate claim, yet not unfounded. The *Pulaski* was a marvel and many, particularly Savannah's elite, were thrilled with the new vessel and her eloquent accommodations. The *Pulaski,* a side-wheeler steam packet, was slated for the Savannah-to-Baltimore run with brief stops in Charleston, South Carolina.

SAVANNAH DEPARTURE

Wednesday morning, June 13, 1838, dawned bright and clear. Scheduled to make her fourth voyage, the *Pulaski* waited patiently in the Savannah River. As the early morning sun gave way to the Savannah humidity, ninety-five passengers boarded, looking forward to a pleasant and enjoyable trip. Among them was Gazaway Lamar, principal owner of the vessel, and his wife, five daughters and his fourteen-year-old son, Charles. Thirty-seven deck hands were at their service, along with Captain Dubois, an experienced and able-bodied seaman.

Arriving at Charleston that evening, the *Pulaski* picked up sixty-five additional passengers and began her run up the Carolina coast. Around ten o'clock that night she began to pitch in rough seas and several passengers began vomiting over her side. Others, with stronger stomachs, bedded down for the night. Though seas were rough, the night sky glistened with summer stars. North Carolina's outer banks should be in sight by morning. But around 11 P.M. an event took place that would alter the destiny of 197 souls.

A NIGHT OF HELL

Without warning, the *Pulaski*'s starboard boiler blew up, sending concussions throughout the ship, shattering the starboard side of her mid-section and sweeping some passengers into the sea. The less fortunate were scalded to death. The bulkhead between the boilers and forward cabins also gave way. As the ship heeled to her starboard side, the Atlantic began to rush in.

First Mate Hibbert, who had taken over the watch at the forecastle around ten o'clock, searched for Captain Dubois, but in vain. Dubois was never seen again, probably blown off the ship. Minutes passed like hours as panicked passengers clad in bedclothes tried to remain alive. After forty minutes, survivors climbed to the promenade deck and huddled, wondering what to do. But the ship began to rip in two as both the bow and the stern rose out of the water, then came crashing down.

Dozens of passengers sought refuge on the extreme part of the bow. Others clung to furniture and wreckage. As the vessel sank, four lifeboats were lowered. Two of the boats capsized, while the other two took on passengers. Only forty-five minutes after the boiler explosion nearly half of the *Pulaski*'s passengers were dead—drowned, scalded, or crushed by falling masts. Others had panicked and jumped overboard.

After searching for survivors for most of the night, passengers in the two lifeboats reluctantly rowed away and set course for the North Carolina shore. But before they made landfall, five unlucky souls drowned when one of the boats capsized within sight of land. The second boat, making way against strong breakers, landed safely.

But there were other survivors still splashing aimlessly in the

Atlantic. Major Heath and Second Captain Pearson lashed together floating wreckage with ropes and fashioned a crude raft, taking twenty-two people on board.

As they tossed about in the open sea, Thursday turned to Friday and Friday to Saturday as they clung to life and any glimmer of hope. Thirst became unbearable, and Heath and Pearson had to forcibly keep others from drinking seawater. Most, with blistered faces, lips, and necks, collapsed. Others, without shirts, baked by day and shivered in the cold at night. On Saturday morning, four more survivors, clinging to wreckage, were plucked from the ocean and climbed aboard the raft.

The first ray of hope appeared when a small dot on the horizon turned out to be the Carolina coastline. Hopes were shattered, however, when strong winds swept the raft out to sea again. Adding insult to injury, a driving rain stung exposed bodies as brisk seas turned into a gale.

Monday morning broke calm and cloudless. By mid-afternoon, four vessels had been spotted, each bringing a measure of optimism, each passing by without notice. Some forlorn survivors, caught in the throws of despair, gave up and prepared for death.

Tuesday morning broke as one weary survivor thought he spotted sails on the horizon. The *Henry Camerdon,* a Wilmington-bound schooner, was making a beeline toward the raft. Finally, the castaways' nightmare drew to an end. The survivors were hauled in, fed, clothed, and nursed back to health.

Meanwhile, another small portion of wreckage was found with four survivors, two of them Savannahians: Gazaway Lamar's son Charles—years later killed in battle during the Civil War—and Robert Hutchinson. Gazaway also survived, but he paid a heavy price in the disaster. Except for his son, he lost his entire family, including his wife, five children and a niece.

AFTERMATH

News of the *Pulaski*'s fate reached Savannah on Thursday, a week after the disaster. Gloom hung over the city for days as friends and relatives waited for casualty reports.

Two days later, news broke that another steam packet, the *New*

York, on her way to Virginia, spotted the tiny raft. But its captain, intent on maintaining his schedule, failed to stop.

By year's end, an inquiry concluded that the explosion was caused by neglect. The *Pulaski's* second engineer permitted water to boil off in the ship's starboard boiler, then let in a fresh supply of water on heated copper, with deadly results.

With steamship fatalities mounting yearly, Congress finally bowed to public pressure and passed regulations governing the inspections of steamers. But for 100 *Pulaski* victims it had come too late.

Winged Death: Savannah's Yellow Fever Epidemics

"**T**O COME IS DEATH!! DEATH!! NOTHING BUT DEATH!" read the headlines in the October 11, 1854, edition of the *Savannah Morning News.* That year Savannah was in the throes of another yellow fever epidemic, also known as the "black vomit." It was the second of three major yellow fever epidemics that the city would suffer in the 19th century. In 1820, 1854, and again in 1876, the fever ravaged the city, bringing suffering, misery, and death to thousands.

Due to its geographic location, with an abundance of surrounding water—marshes, rivers, and streams—Savannah was the perfect breeding ground for the *aedes aegypti,* commonly called the mosquito. And the relatively level topography that surrounds the city's center meant that stagnant water was common. Add the fact that 19th century Savannah was largely dependent on international shipping, which left it vulnerable to disease brought by sailors from foreign ports, and the all the ingredients were in place for major health catastrophes.

A KILLER

The first major yellow fever outbreak occurred in 1820. Earlier that year a fire had devastated much of the city, razing 500 buildings

In this cemetery many victims of the
Great Yellow Fever Epidemic
of 1820
were buried.

Nearly 700 Savannahians died
that year, including two local
physicians who lost their lives
caring for the stricken.

Several epidemics followed. In 1854
The Savannah Benevolent Association
was organized to aid the families
of the fever victims.

Plaque in Colonial Cemetery honoring Savannah's 1820
yellow fever victims. (Photo courtesy Henderson Studios,
Savannah)

and homes. Destroyed, burned-out buildings coupled with heavy rains created ripe conditions for mosquito breeding.

The first outbreak of yellow fever that year began in August and lasted through mid-October. At the beginning of the fever's outbreak, Savannah's population numbered around 15,000. Within two months all but 6,000 had evacuated.

Other sources cite a smaller population, but still indicate that the majority of Savannahians fled harm's way. As cold weather approached, the fever finally subsided. But it claimed nearly 700 lives.

SYMPTOMS

Contracting a serious disease, particularly yellow fever, in those days almost always meant a certain painful and particularly hideous death. The first symptom noticed would be a fever. Soon, chills began and you would become bedridden. As high fevers zapped your strength, severe back pain ensued and you would develop jaundice—a yellowing of the skin and whites of the eyes, hence the name yellow fever.

Uncontrollable hemorrhaging from your nose, gums, and stomach followed. Then vomiting began, usually a dark black color. In the terminal/final stage, delirium and convulsions plagued many. Finally, you would lapse into a coma. And if you didn't die from the disease, you still weren't off the hook. Numerous cases were reported of people in comas being mistaken for dead and being quickly buried—alive! Approximately 60 percent of yellow fever victims died.

The second major yellow fever epidemic in Savannah broke out in 1854. Like the 1820 epidemic, it, too, began in August and lasted until the autumn chill killed the mosquitoes.

Prominent citizens who could afford it fled the city at the first mention of the dreaded disease. Left behind were the less fortunate: Irish immigrants, sailors, blacks, and visitors. Just the mention of the name—yellow fever—would send a city into panic. That year yellow fever claimed over 1,000 Savannahians, ushering in a national call to find a cure.

SEARCHING FOR ANSWERS

A handful of dedicated Savannah physicians usually stayed behind to take care of the sick and dying during outbreaks. But some of them also contracted the disease and died.

Dr. Richard Arnold, named the hero of the 1854 epidemic, worked virtually around the clock caring for those in need. At the time he wrote: "For six weeks my average sleep is four and a half hours in the 24. I am in the buggy, except for meals, from 6 A.M. to midnight."

Not only was Dr. Arnold deemed the hero of the 1854 epidemic, but he later became head of the American Medical Association, trying desperately to find a solution to the problem. But medical research was still in the dark ages. While many worked tirelessly for an answer, their efforts proved fruitless.

One theory claimed that vapors from nearby swamps and marshes carried the sickness. All thought that the condition was contagious, adding to widespread panic. Only years later did they learn it was not communicable.

Ignorant of the disease's origins, physicians prescribed remedies that were little more than ridiculous. Some advocated the application of rags dipped in vinegar, while others thought that sniffing pieces of camphor would help. A few mixed lemon juice, salt, soapsuds, molasses, quinine, and soda. Some used snuff, others stuffed garlic in their shoes. A number of physicians prescribed opium and marijuana. Citizens were known to fire muskets into the air to try to ward off the disease. And, at least on one occasion, the local militia rolled out its cannon and fired several volleys down the streets in an effort to render the air "pure."

Within a few years, the medical community narrowed the list of the disease's possible culprits. Dr. Josiah Nott of Mobile, Alabama, developed a theory of infection by insect transmission. Dr. Arnold substantiated his claims. But it would be years, and at least for Savannah, one more major epidemic before real answers provided relief.

FINAL PLAGUE

The 1876 plague followed the same pattern as earlier epidemics. This one started in the heat of August and subsided when fall temperatures brought in cold air. By September 4, Savannah resembled a ghost town. Businesses were closed and even city government virtually ceased to exist. Entire blocks of homes became vacant as more and more fled the city. By the end of the epidemic, 1,066 Savannahians had perished.

A SOLUTION

In the 1880s, Cuban physician Carlos Finlay proposed the mosquito as the cause of the disease. People contract yellow fever from the bite of the infected female mosquito, Finlay claimed.

By 1900, the U.S. Yellow Fever Commission verified his findings. Since then, mosquito control and immunization have eliminated the disease in North America. But the scourge still thrives in Africa and South America, inflicting misery, heartache, and death.

Sherman in Savannah

The *Savannah Republican* called them "desperately jaded men and animals." The southern populace wasn't so kind. But they were coming and nothing could stop them. Atlanta had already fallen, and now Savannah stood in their path. Sixty thousand battle-hardened veterans were marching this way.

As Sherman's army completed its destructive March to the Sea, Savannah prepared the best she could. Yet all she could muster to greet the coming Blue hosts was a ragtag force of men, mostly boys too young for conscription, old men, the walking wounded, and small groups of army regulars.

And the commander of Savannah's defenses, Gen. William J. Hardee, determined to make a stand, or at least to pretend to do so.

On December 8, 1864, Sherman reached Pooler, 8 miles from Savannah. On the 9th, the first Union troops reached Savannah's defenses. The next day Sherman's entire force invaded the area. Facing them were roughly 10,000 Rebel troops spread thinly across a 15-mile defensive perimeter.

STANDING THEIR GROUND

After a visit to Savannah, Gen. P.G.T. Beauregard—Hardee's commander—instructs Hardee to preserve his command at all costs, including the evacuation of the city. The much-needed troops will be called on again if Sherman is to meet any resistance as he swings into Carolina. The troops are deemed more valuable than the city. With the city invested and flanked on every side but the north, the Savannah River and the Plank Road on the South Carolina shore is the only escape route.

On the 11th the pop of musket fire and the crack of small arms is heard as Confederate and Union troops skirmish along the defensive arch. As the Union command holds a council of war, its troops dig in and wait for orders.

To establish communication with the Union fleet anchored in Wassau Sound and open the path to the sea, Union forces make quick work of Fort McAllister's defenders, seizing the fort in just fifteen minutes.

Gen. William Tecumseh Sherman. (Photo courtesy Library of Congress)

On the 17th formal communication between generals Sherman and Hardee begin. Through a flag of truce sent to the Rebel lines, Sherman demands surrender, stating: "[We] shall wait for a reasonable time for your answer before opening with heavy ordnance."

Yet Hardee plays the fox, buying precious time. "Your statement that you have, for some days, held every avenue by which the people and garrison can be supplied, is incorrect," he replies. "I am in constant communication with my department."

Though Hardee refuses to capitulate, Sherman postpones the siege. For the first time since the beginning of his destructive march from Atlanta, he hesitates. Later in his memoirs he justifies his actions, claiming that the "ground was difficult" and that similar assaults had all "proved so bloody" that he "concluded to make one more effort to completely surround Savannah on all sides."

But not all of Sherman's generals had the jitters. Corps commander Gen. Henry W. Sloculm is adamant to his commander: "Damn it, let us take this plank road and shut the fellows in!" Sloculm wanted to land troops across the Savannah to prevent Hardee's escape.

Sherman considers the situation, but waffles. He inflates Confederate numbers, placing them at 15,000, along with what he described as "good artillerists." Adding to Sherman's hesitation, two Confederate ironclads, the *CSS Savannah* and the *CSS Georgia,* as well as two gunboats lie waiting in the Savannah River.

In a letter to General Grant, updating him on the situation, Sherman writes that he intends to bomb the city, but "not risk the lives of our men by assaults across the narrow causeways."

Finally, on December 19, Sherman agrees to send troops across the Savannah River, but the force is small and quickly contained by Gen. "Fightin' Joe" Wheeler's Confederate cavalry. Sloculm presses for more troops, but Sherman vacillates. He eventually withdraws the 1,500 he has already dispatched, saying that he wanted his army to remain intact in case they were called to Virginia to join forces with Grant.

Capitalizing on Sherman's indecision, Hardee has already begun construction of pontoon bridges to span the Savannah River. The first stretches from the foot of West Broad (now Martin Luther King Jr. Boulevard) and reaches 1,000 feet across to Hutchinson Island. A second bridge spans the distance from Hutchinson Island to Pennyworth Island, and the third stretches across the Back River to South Carolina.

THE EVACUATION

On the night of December 20, the first of Hardee's troops begin to cross the river. Straw is put down to muffle the sound of horses and wagons and a heavy barrage of Confederate artillery booms in the distance to cover the withdrawal and to keep Federal troops pinned down. Cannon that couldn't be taken are spiked and ammunition is dumped into the river.

As the last of the Southern troops cross into Carolina, a reluctant crew scuttles the *Georgia* near Fort Jackson. The *Savannah* decides to fight her way out of the harbor and make it to sea, but she, too, would have to be scuttled. And a skeleton force of Rebel soldiers keeps the campfires on the defensive lines alive to make the Federals believe that the trenches are still occupied.

It is a ruse, a gamble—but it works. The next morning a few Federal infantrymen cautiously raise their heads to look out over the trenches. They are joined by more curious soldiers. When they muster the courage to climb out of the trenches and walk to the Rebel lines, they are in for a shock. Nothing remains but smoldering campfires. The Rebel army has vanished.

General Sherman is making his way back from Hilton Head and a conference with General Foster about the Savannah situation when informed of the evacuation. Stranded on a mud bar, he transfers boats and finally returns to camp. He voices his disappointment in several letters, and later in his memoirs.

If Sherman was disappointed, Secretary of War Edwin Stanton was furious. He stated: "It is a sore disappointment that Hardee was able to get off his fifteen thousand from Sherman's sixty thousand. It looks like protracting the war while the armies continue to escape."

Stanton was right. Sherman would meet Hardee and his men again in Bentonville, North Carolina, on March 19, 1865, and fight the last major battle of the Civil War. Though he would be victorious and help bring the war to a close, he would suffer over 1,600 casualties from a foe that he had let escape.

Politics and Corruption

If politics today are distasteful, with public mistrust, a recently impeached president, and lack of voter confidence, they hardly compare with the politics of our Founding Fathers, where corruption cast an ugly shadow on the national landscape. Contrary to what most of us learned in school, the cradle of our democracy was born out of a den of political iniquity.

And Georgia's political heritage didn't escape unscathed, either. It is rife with tales of political corruption, vote tampering, intimidation, Congressional hearings, impeachments, and intrigue.

From 1789 to 1790, shortly after the end of the Revolution, the nation's first Congress resided in New York City. Comprising Georgia's 1st Congressional District, often called the lower or eastern district, were five counties: Chatham, Liberty, Effingham, Glynn, and Camden. The district's first representative was Gen. James Jackson.

Already known in the area as a Revolutionary War hero, general of the Georgia state militia, and successful antagonist of the Yazoo land scandal, Jackson was a striking figure. A fiery orator, he had a reputation for taking no political captives. Even his friends and supporters admitted that he always dared to speak his mind and was wholly intolerant of his opponents. Adding to the fray was his reputation as Savannah's most noted duelist. Described as "fearless in politics as in battle," Jackson was a force to be reckoned with.

Jackson was first elected as an anti-Federalist, an opponent of the Federalist Party—the party led by Alexander Hamilton, James Madison, and John Jay who favored a strong federal government. Because Jackson opposed Hamilton's plan for financing the government with debt as well as other Federalist policies, his political antagonists grew.

Consequently, it was no surprise when opposition sprang up in his bid for reelection in 1791. The forces against Jackson, both shrewd and unscrupulous, chose another, even more popular war hero, Gen. "Mad Anthony" Wayne, to oppose him. Named "Mad Anthony" for his daring on the battlefield, Wayne had served in the Pennsylvania state assembly. He fought the entire seven years of the war all the way from Quebec to Savannah, most of the time leading Georgia troops. For his services to the nation, Congress awarded Wayne a plantation near Savannah. A friend of George Washington and Gen. Nathanael Greene, Wayne was also Jackson's former commander.

Despite Wayne's fame, with an honest election Jackson was the probable winner. This fact didn't escape the attention of Wayne's campaign, led by Henry Osborne, judge of the Superior Court of the 8th Circuit, and Thomas Gibbons, a shrewd politician and soon-to-be Savannah mayor. Both men were proponents of Hamilton's policies and personally benefited from them. Both realized that Jackson could only be defeated by dishonest means.

Both sides squared off on election day. But Jackson, either ignorant of his intended political demise or not taking it seriously, was away on an extended trip. In Chatham and Liberty counties, honest elections were held—but not so in the district's other counties. In Camden County, voting was held at Saint Patrick, a small outpost, not much more than a clearing in the forest, on the Santilla River. Only seventy votes were up for grabs in the entire county and the small, scattered population was mostly indifferent because they thought Jackson would easily win.

UNSCRUPULOUS MEN

The election managers in Camden were idle men known for swapping stories, shooting all day, and drinking liquor. When polls opened that day, someone suggested that all the votes be cast for Wayne. But Camden's sheriff was on hand to maintain order. By sunset, however, with only forty of seventy voters polled, Sheriff Smith left for home. Coming down river with a delegation of eight men, two presumed to be soldiers, Judge Osborne appeared. He quickly ordered the polls to re-open, and the group cast votes for Wayne, stuffed the ballot box, and voted for those who had failed to vote.

After Osborne's tampering, a tally was taken: 79 votes for Wayne and 10 for Jackson. Osborne certified the ballots to Governor Telfair as the official return. But upon closer examination, the Camden returns showed pencil erasures and recast votes in Osborne's own handwriting.

Over in Effingham County, Gibbons was more discreet. While he didn't use outright coercion, his manipulation was just as effective. Plenty of liquor flowed at the polls that day. And reports came in that most voters were drunk by eleven o'clock that morning.

Gibbons pressured Nathaniel Hudson, who had been named election magistrate but not approved by the legislature, to preside over the election. And Thomas Lane, Effingham's sheriff, was paid to transport the returns to Augusta, where Governor Telfair waited to make the official count.

In Glynn County, where Jackson was favored, no manipulation was reported, but somehow Osborne obtained the ballots and they failed to reach Augusta in time to be counted. With votes from four counties, two of them fraudulent, Governor Telfair tallied the votes. On January 27, 1791, Wayne was declared the winner. At first, Jackson accepted the defeat, stating: "[I have] retired from public life with a pleasant satisfaction of having done my duty."

But his supporters were not so docile. They began combing the counties looking for evidence of wrongdoing. Not only was there evidence, but there was enough corruption to impeach a superior court judge, bring national attention, and incriminate the highest public officials.

As Jackson's supporters combed Camden and Effingham counties for evidence of voter manipulation, President George Washington was due to visit Savannah on the Georgia leg of his historic southern tour.

Unbelievably, both sides agreed to set aside the growing political war until Washington left. After the president returned to Virginia, Jackson's supporters fired the first shot. They gathered affidavits of fraud and presented them to grand juries in all of the district's five counties. The juries, controlled by the Jackson faction, made quick action of denouncing the election and demanding legal action.

In Savannah, Gibbons was named the city's second mayor by the City Council only ninety days after the election. One of his first public statements was to congratulate General Jackson "on his return to Georgia and domestic enjoyment" and "thanks for his patriotic exertion."

POLITICAL WAR

Jackson continued to hold his peace but finally on July 28 came out swinging. On that day the *Georgia Gazette* ran Jackson's entire story on its front page. His supporters were relieved that the general had finally decided to fight, but most voters, who had no idea of what happened, were shocked.

Claiming to be the winner with 273 votes to Wayne's 214, Jackson implicated Wayne's campaign managers, drawing national attention. A majority of Camden voters signed a petition protesting the count in their county as having five times more votes as registered voters. In Liberty County, a grand jury denounced the Camden and Effingham elections as illegal. Cries for impeachment, even imprisonment, came from all corners of the district.

Jackson, in a bitter correspondence in the *Augusta Chronicle,* pressed the attack. Finally, in November, ten months after the election, Jackson presented his evidence to the Georgia General Assembly and demanded Osborne's impeachment. With Jackson's political allies in power in the state house, articles of impeachment were soon drawn up and delivered to the state senate. The articles of impeachment claimed that Osborne had destroyed the original returns and created new and false returns and forwarded the returns to the governor, thus corrupting "the very foundation of government."

POLITICAL CONSEQUENCES

Acting on the advice of Thomas P. Carnes, state attorney general, and John Neal, solicitor general, and bowing to public pressure, Governor Telfair suspended Osborne from office. Osborne's defenders claimed that only Congress could try Osborne and only a federal court could find him guilty. But their words fell on deaf ears. Osborne was impeached.

Not only was Osborne removed from office, but he was fined and prohibited from holding public office again in Georgia for thirty years. Meanwhile, Gibbons was starting to have problems of his own.

Having secured Osborne's conviction and a note of thanks from a partisan legislature, Jackson turned his energies toward the federal government, now residing in Philadelphia. Yet, by a vote of 41 to 20, Congress refused to admit the proceedings from the Georgia legislature.

Jackson continued to press, but at no time did he attack Wayne, who by most accounts was an unwilling pawn in a game of political chess.

In a public denouncement, Jackson wrote that Gibbons' soul was a faction whose life was a source of political corruption. At the request of the state assembly, Jackson apologized for his remarks but quickly added that Gibbons' proofs of guilt grew out of an "abominable corruption."

Outraged, Gibbons demanded satisfaction and requested a duel. On the morning of March 19, on the Carolina side of the Savannah River, both men slowly marched thirty paces. Turning, they fired their black powder pistols.

Neither was hit.

But Jackson exclaimed: "Damn it, Gibbons, you're a brave man and a good marksman, for I believe your ball hit my pistol."

Gibbons responded: "You are a brave man General Jackson."

This was the first of two duels in as many weeks for Gibbons. Confronted on all sides and bloodied by allegations, he would soon resign as Savannah's mayor.

Congress finally voted on a resolution to restore Jackson to Congress, but the vote split, 29 to 29. Casting the deciding vote was speaker of the house and member of the Federalist Party Jonathan Trumbull. Voting in the negative, Trumbull denied Jackson his congressional seat. Another resolution was passed declaring vacant the seat of Anthony Wayne.

But the seat remained unoccupied, neither Jackson nor Wayne having the stomach to run again. It was finally filled by John Milledge, Jackson's friend. Milledge would rise through the political ranks, becoming Georgia's governor from 1802 to 1806.

AFTERMATH

For Wayne's part, he always had a difficult time believing that his supporters were capable of such dishonesty and breach of public trust. In 1792, he was named major general and commander in chief of the Western Army by President Washington. He died three years later, broken by the whole affair.

The Federalist Party, once the epitome of power in American politics and the nation's first political party, dwindled rapidly. By the mid-1820s, it ceased to exist.

Osborne was ruined, at least politically, and no mention is made of him again in the public records. But General Jackson's political star continued to shine; he retained his enormous popularity—as well as his enemies—becoming Georgia's governor in 1798 and serving until 1802.

The Mighty 8th Air Force

With only three experienced flyers, the 8th Army Air Force was born in Savannah on January 28, 1942, in the National Guard Armory on Bull Street, near Forsyth Park. The unit consisted of seventy-four officers and eighty-one enlisted men, a tiny force for the task that lay ahead, but their numbers would soon grow to unprecedented proportion.

The officers and crew trained at Hunter Army Airfield, Savannah's new air base named in honor of World War I flying ace and Savannah native Frank O'Driscoll Hunter. In just two months, however, the 8th headquarters were relocated to England to prepare to battle the Nazi war machine.

OPERATIONS

From Savannah and other American bases, B-17s and B-24 heavy bombers began arriving in England, first as a trickle, then in droves. Finally combat ready, the 8th would soon taste battle.

On August 8, 1942, a squadron of its fighters launched offensive sweeps against Nazi-held positions along the French coastline. Nine days later, 12 four-engine B-17 Flying Fortresses carried out the first all-American bombing mission against occupied Europe. Beefing up their numbers by 1943, the 8th launched thousands of

B-17s and B-24 sorties, dropping tons of bombs in an all-out aerial blitz.

But with the short-range P-47 escort fighters providing air cover for only half the journey before having to turn back to their bases in England, the bombers took a beating. Swarms of eager Messerschmitt-109 fighters swarmed like bees, picking off stragglers and sending countless bombers and young crewmen to a fiery death.

But by 1944, the tide of the air war finally shifted. The P-51 Mustang, a long-range fighter capable of escorting the bombers to Berlin and back, emerged. Soon, the 8th Air Force owned the skies, out-flying and out-dog-fighting Hitler's once proud and defiant Luftwaffe. With the P-51 and the twin-engine P-38 Lightning providing an umbrella of aerial protection, American bombers pounded German industrial sites by day while British bombers reduced her cities to rubble by night.

The same year, the 8th Air Force—numbering nearly 200,000 airmen—had already dropped 46,840 tons of bombs on Nazi-occupied Europe and downed or destroyed 4,446 German planes. But the wages of war are death, and the 8th continued to suffer horrific casualties. By mid-1944 it had lost a staggering 1,130 heavy bombers and 185 fighter planes.

There was more to come. The last year of the war also proved the cruelest as Hitler's legions, still numbering four million men in arms, dug in their heels. It would take the obliteration of the German homeland before they would capitulate.

Walter Cronkite, a young United Press International reporter, covered much of the 8th's action in Europe and flew on several missions. On the 8th Air Force's second birthday, he wrote, "The kid [the 8th] who is two years old today has raised more hell than ever its parents believed possible."

During the height of the war, an average of 1,200 8th Air Force aircraft took to the skies on daily bombing raids. The 8th could put 2,000 bombers in the air and scramble 1,000 fighters on any given day, earning the nickname "the Mighty 8th."

Not only did the 8th fight in the European Theater, but also saw action in North Africa, the Mediterranean, and the Pacific.

It was the 17th Bombardment Group of the 8th that furnished the planes and crews that flew from the carrier *Hornet* on Gen. Jimmy Doolittle's famous Tokyo bombing raid, bringing the war to the Japanese mainland.

THE COST OF VICTORY

By war's end the 8th had lost close to 9,000 bombers and suffered 47,000 casualties. Twenty-six thousand airmen were killed in action and another 28,000 served time in Nazi prisoner-of-war camps. The planes of the 8th Air Force dropped a total of 701,330 tons of bombs on occupied Europe, including 531,771 tons on targets in Germany. They downed, or destroyed on the ground, 15,439 enemy aircraft, more than all other American air forces in Europe and North Africa combined.

Seventeen members of the 8th won the nation's highest military award, the Congressional Medal of Honor. Two hundred twenty members won the Distinguished Service Cross, and 850 Silver Stars were awarded, along with 7000 Purple Hearts and 46,000 Distinguished Flying Crosses. The unit produced 261 aces, with 31 having 15 or more direct kills each. In the greatest air armada in history, 350,000 personnel served with the 8th in the European Theater by 1945.

"Shoeless" Joe Jackson's Savannah Days and the Black Sox Scandal

"All I know is Joe was exonerated in the trial. It irks and irritates me when people rant and rave about Pete Rose not being in the Hall of Fame—not until Joe gets there first," says Maggi Hall of Savannah, the eighty-seven-year-old niece of baseball legend "Shoeless" Joe Jackson.

Few stories are as bittersweet as Jackson's rise to baseball stardom and his subsequent banishment from the game he played so well.

"Shoeless" Joe Jackson as a member of the Chicago White
Sox. (Photo courtesy Maggi Hall)

Jackson was a baseball enigma from an early age. Born into relative poverty just outside Greenville, South Carolina, he was working twelve-hour days in the local textile mill by age thirteen. With no other opportunities, Joe took to the field. He starting playing for the mill team as a boy, then played semi-professional ball, and by age nineteen got his first break. A Greenville sportswriter spotted the gangly 6-foot-1-inch Jackson in a game, noticed his talent, and wrote a story about him for the Greenville newspaper.

Jackson signed with the Class D Greenville Spinners of the Carolina Association for $75 a month in 1908. By the end of the season, he led the league in hitting with a .354 average, drawing the attention of Connie Mack, owner and manager of the Philadelphia Athletics. Mack bought Jackson's contract for $325 at the end of the 1908 season and called him up to play for the A's. In his big-league debut, Jackson smashed three hits.

PLAYING FOR SAVANNAH

In 1909, Jackson traveled south to play for the Savannah Indians, a Class C minor-league club in the Sally League. (Professional baseball in Savannah was initially played at Bolton Park on Henry Street, then Municipal Stadium, from 1927 to 1940; it has been played at Grayson Stadium since 1941.)

The Indians opened the season in Jacksonville, but lost their first game. Fans in Savannah, however, anticipated the return of their team and the heralded Jackson. For his part, Joe didn't let Savannah down.

In his first 80 plate appearances, he blasted 36 hits for a .450 batting average. He even pitched in a game against the Macon Peaches, going three innings, giving up only one hit and striking out three batters.

Not only did Joe become a Savannah favorite, but made the Sally League all-star team, a unanimous pick for centerfield. One local sportswriter wrote: "Joe is a sensation in all departments of the great American game—and that's saying a whole lot."

The right-handed centerfielder batted .358 in 118 games, leading the Sally League in hitting and endearing himself to a generation of Savannah baseball fans.

After playing a handful of games for the A's during the last part of the 1909 season, Jackson spent the next year in the Southern League with the New Orleans Pelicans. In July, however, Connie Mack traded Jackson to Cleveland, where the Carolina native hit .387 in 20 games, drawing national attention.

JOE COMES OF AGE

In 1911, Jackson came of age, posting a blistering .408 batting average in his rookie season—second only to Ty Cobb's .420 average.

Called a natural phenomenon with a swing that Babe Ruth admittedly emulated, Joe played three more seasons for the Indians, hitting .395, .373, and .338, before being traded midway through the 1915 season to the Chicago White Sox.

Jackson led the White Sox to the World Series in 1917, capturing the Series four games to two over the New York Giants. He hit .307 in the six Series games, with seven hits, two runs batted in, and spectacular play in the field. Savannah, where Joe and wife Katie bought a house on the waterfront a year before, honored Joe's heroics with spontaneous celebrations.

With America entrenched in the war in Europe in 1918, Joe opted for the "work or fight" order and secured a job at a shipbuilding company in Wilmington, Delaware. By 1919, with the armistice in effect, Joe was back on the baseball field. But unbeknown to him his troubles were just starting.

PRELUDE TO DISASTER

Professional baseball in 1919 was problematic. Because of the war, attendance had been poor in 1918, resulting in reduced salaries the next year. And baseball—already America's favorite past time—was becoming intertwined with professional gambling.

President and owner of the Chicago White Sox Charles Comiskey was a hard-hitting, tight-fisted miser who slashed his players' salaries even lower. The White Sox, arguably the best team in baseball, earned 30 percent less than the average baseball salary, ripe picking for professional gamblers. Still, they won the American League pennant with an 88-52 record.

The Sox entered the 1919 World Series heavily favored over

their National League counterparts, the Cincinnati Reds. A group of gamblers, however, had other ideas.

They approached several White Sox players with propositions to throw the Series. For each lost game, $20,000 would be divided among the eight conspiring players. But the gamblers lost most of the cash on other bets and failed to come through when the Sox entered game six trailing the Reds four games to one.

The Sox retaliated, winning games six and seven. The gamblers persisted, resorting to death threats if the players refused to stay in line. Lefty Williams, starting pitcher for game eight, was told that his wife would die if he didn't lose the game. He complied. The White Sox lost the Series five games to three. It was a black day in baseball.

The White Sox opened the 1920 season with a bang, and by late summer were in a three-way pennant race with the Indians and New York Yankees. But as the team jockeyed for the pennant, rumors persisted. In September, a Chicago grand jury convened to investigate. They indicted eight White Sox players—ace pitcher Eddie Cicotte, hurler Lefty Williams, third baseman Buck Weaver, second-stringer Fred McMullin, first baseman Chick Gandil, shortstop Swede Risberg, and outfielders Happy Felsch and Joe Jackson—for conspiracy. The event was deemed the Black Sox Scandal and the name has stuck.

On hearing of the indictment, Jackson and Eddie Cicotte were persuaded to sign statements granting them immunity from prosecution. But it was a ruse. The two players didn't know they were signing confession statements. Neither was represented by counsel.

Sketchy, unconfirmed details of the so-called grand jury confessions made the newspapers and to this day add to the confusion surrounding the case.

In 1921, the eight were charged with conspiracy and brought to trial. On August 8, a jury acquitted them of any wrongdoing. But newly appointed baseball commissioner Kenesaw Mountain Landis, setting a no-tolerance policy on gambling in professional baseball, suspended the eight from the game, then banned them for life.

"Regardless of the verdict of juries," he said,

no player that throws a ball game; no player that undertakes or promises to throw a ball game; no player that sits in a conference with a bunch of crooked players and gamblers where the ways and means of throwing games are planned and discussed and does not promptly tell his club about it, will ever play professional baseball.

Since that time, enough contradictory material has been compiled to offer support for varying theories, many using the leaked and unconfirmed grand jury reports as evidence.

Several concrete facts remain, however. Except for Jackson's signed "confession," which he was led to believe would grant him immunity from prosecution, nowhere did Joe indicate what he had done, if anything, to help throw the Series. His play certainly proved his point. He hit the only home run of the Series, batted .375, and played flawlessly in the field.

Other players also testified on his behalf. They confirmed that Joe had not attended any meetings between the players and professional gamblers. Though Joe knew of the fix, he refused to accept cash on two separate occasions: $10,000 prior to game one, and $20,000 during the Series.

Not only did Joe refuse the payoff, but he asked to be benched to avoid any suspicion that he was involved in the scheme; his request was denied.

After the Series, pitcher Lefty Williams offered Joe an envelope containing $5,000 cash; Joe refused it. After arguing, Williams threw the money at Joe's feet and left. Joe took the money and tried to turn it in to White Sox owner Comiskey, but was turned away. Later that night Joe left for Georgia to spend the winter.

RETURNING TO SAVANNAH

After the Black Sox Scandal, Jackson returned to Savannah with his wife and lived in an apartment at 143 Abercorn Street. He then moved to a new bungalow on 1411 East 39th Street that Hall's father had built.

Jackson opened and ran a dry cleaning business at 119 Drayton Street. It wasn't long, however, before Joe was offered money to play ball again. He first played semi-professional ball in New Jersey in 1922 under an alias, but his identity was quickly discovered after brilliant performances at the plate. The next year he played for an Americus, Georgia, team in the South Georgia League, a semi-professional league not under Landis' jurisdiction.

UNCLE JOE

Maggi Hall's memory of Joe Jackson, whom she still affectionately calls "Uncle Joe," has little to do with baseball, other than a firm belief that he was unjustly banned from the game. Instead, she remembers a kind, gentle man.

"I would go to his store on Drayton Street after school," Hall said, " and he'd give me a quarter to clean up for him."

Jackson also spent considerable time at the Hall residence at 409 East 49th Street, just across the street from where Hall currently lives.

According to Hall, East 49th Street in the 1920s sat at the edge of town. Her family had a yard full of chickens, a chicken coop on one side of the yard, and a duck yard on the other.

"One Saturday, Joe was supposed to clean the duck yard and me the chicken yard," Hall said, "but we always fought about who would clean which part of the yard."

In 1929, Joe and Katie returned to Greenville, South Carolina, where Joe continued to play semi-pro baseball. In 1932, he signed with the Greenville Spinners, earning $100 a game during the throes of the Great Depression. He also ran a barbeque restaurant and a liquor store. He suffered his fourth heart attack in 1951 and died at age sixty-two.

FINAL VERDICT

Joe hit over .300 in eleven out of thirteen major league seasons and batted .382 his last year in the big leagues. His .356 lifetime batting average ranks third on the all-time list, but he remains ineligible for induction into the National Baseball Hall of Fame in Cooperstown, New York.

A push to reinstate Jackson surfaced in the late 1990s. The South Carolina General Assembly passed a resolution in 1998 requesting that Joe Jackson be restored as a member in good standing in professional baseball, thereby qualifying him for induction into Cooperstown.

In 1999, U.S. Sen. Strom Thurmond petitioned baseball commissioner Bud Selig to reinstate Joe. And a growing number of web sites have been recently posted, arguing on Joe's behalf.

After all is said and done, it appears that Joe's worst sin was knowing of the fix and not reporting it. Perhaps baseball's grand old man, Connie Mack, had it right when years after the scandal he said: "Jackson's fall from grace is one of the real tragedies of baseball. I always thought he was more sinned against than sinning."

Nixon Visits Savannah

Georgia Gov. Lester Maddox was furious. The outspoken, fiery, and often controversial little governor had been left out in the cold. The president of the United States had already accepted an invitation to visit the Peach State, and preparations had been made, before word reached Maddox.

In the fall of 1970, the Georgia Republican Party invited then-President Richard Milhous Nixon to Savannah for an October 8 visit, stating that the presidential visit would coincide with the dedication of the new marine research facilities on Skidaway Island. Maddox strongly disagreed. He contended that the trip, coming less than a month before Georgia's November 3, 1970, gubernatorial election, was purely political, an obvious attempt to boost support for Republican gubernatorial candidate Hal Suit. Running against Suit was the soft-spoken peanut farmer from Plains, Georgia, democratic candidate James Earl "Jimmy" Carter.

NIXON'S VISIT

With Air Force One still about an hour away, an eager White House press corps, local media, and dignitaries gathered near the runway at Hunter Army Airfield to wait for the president's arrival. And Maddox, on hand for the event, seized the day, giving both national and local media an ear full. One reporter asked the governor if Nixon's visit was political.

"You know it is man," Maddox responded." Why sure a feller'd have to be stupid not to see this."

"The president had to have some excuse to come," he continued. "He's here for purely political reasons. When national politicians come in, we should do our best to defeat whoever they come in to help."

Complaining that the trip cost the taxpayers $250,000, Maddox said that the money would have been better used on the marine research facilities. He also questioned the timing of the visit, since construction on the island's facilities had not yet started.

An hour later, at noon, Air Force One touched down and Nixon emerged, well tanned and relaxed, accompanied by wife Pat, daughter Julie Nixon Eisenhower, and son-in-law David Eisenhower.

Gen. James C. Smith, commander of Hunter Army Airfield and Fort Stewart, was the first to shake hands with the president. Maddox, next in line, greeted Nixon cordially, holding his peace, at least for the time being. On Maddox's heels followed an eager Hal Suit, overjoyed to have the president make a political visit on his behalf.

Peppered with questions from reporters about the political nature of his visit, Nixon remained silent. But when asked about his latest peace proposal to end the fighting in Vietnam, he responded eagerly.

After greeting a group of Vietnamese student helicopter pilots and praising the joint American-Vietnamese training program at Hunter, Nixon climbed into the presidential limousine and was whisked away. Exiting the base, the motorcade sped down Lynes Parkway toward downtown Savannah and an estimated 100,000 people waiting for him on Broughton Street.

As the presidential motorcade turned onto Broughton, eager crowds spilled into the streets. Police on motorcycles nearby rushed in to maintain control.

As the crowd thickened, the motorcade slowed, and Nixon reached out and began shaking hands. In the limousine immediately behind the president sat a frustrated Maddox and a jubilant Hal Suit, followed by a continuous line of limousines, motorcycle cops, and state patrol cars.

But the main action was yet to come. Thousands ran after the motorcade as it approached the corner of Bull and Broughton.

Hundreds more closed in from both sides. Alarmed, Secret Service agents struggled to maintain order. As the motorcade crawled to a near halt, Nixon jumped out and stood on the hood of his car, raising both hands triumphantly in the air and making peace signs to the enthusiastic crowd.

Not to be outdone, Maddox bolted from his vehicle and began walking down Broughton Street, unescorted. He, too, reached into the crowd, shaking hands, holding children, and smiling for cameras, before finally being corralled by state patrolmen and escorted back to his car.

From Broughton Street, the motorcade headed to East Broad Street, down Islands Expressway, and finally stopped at the Savannah Yacht Club.

After a brief address at the Yacht Club, Nixon boarded the Royal Eagle for the short trip to Skidaway Island. Trailing behind was a small flotilla of media, security agents, and well-wishers.

On Skidaway Island, Nixon addressed 800 carefully chosen politicians and GOP supporters. In a twenty-seven-minute oration, the president praised the oceanographic center, denounced the evils of pollution, spoke of the promise of ocean exploration, and refuted allegations about the political nature of his visit

After his speech, Nixon unveiled a dedication plaque, worked the crowds, and boarded the presidential helicopter for the brief flight back to Hunter. Soon, he and his family were on their way to Florida for a vacation.

Among the crowd at Skidaway Island that day stood Savannah's newly elected mayor, John P. Rousakis, sworn in just three days earlier. Speaking to reporters after the event, Rousakis said he was proud of Savannah and the support shown to the president regardless of any political differences that might have existed.

POLITICAL FATE

As Nixon left the area, few could have guessed how fate would forever forge the destiny of the politicians connected with that day.

Hal Suit, despite Nixon's endorsement, suffered a crushing defeat by Jimmy Carter in the November 3 gubernatorial election. Four years later, Nixon became the first president in U.S. history to resign from office, doing so under a growing cloud of controversy over his alleged involvement in the Watergate burglary.

Before resigning, however, Nixon struck a deal for clemency with his soon-to-be successor, Vice President Gerald R. Ford. After less than a month in office, Ford made good on the deal, granting Nixon a presidential pardon, thus protecting him from all future criminal indictments associated with the Watergate scandal.

But the unpopular pardon cost Ford his own presidency. In two years he would be narrowly defeated by the soft-spoken peanut farmer from Georgia, the very man Nixon tried to keep out of the Georgia governor's mansion in 1970.

The Controversial Story of the Slave Ship *Wanderer*

In 1858, on the South Georgia coast, a group of four men defied the U.S. government and its laws by illegally landing slaves in the only large-scale slaving expedition after the slave trade was outlawed in 1818. Although the landing took place 60 miles south of Savannah near Brunswick, the center of the ensuing controversy was Savannah.

Earlier that year four men—Richard Dickerson of Richmond, Virginia, Benjamin Davis of Charleston, South Carolina, A.C. McGehee of Columbus, Georgia, and Charles Lamar of Savannah— had bought the luxury yacht *Wanderer.* Though she was built for sailing and racing, the new owners had other intentions.

After the *Wanderer* sailed from her New York berth, she made port in Brunswick, Georgia, under a cloud of suspicion. Lamar, a known advocate of restarting the slave trade, had already tried to outfit a slaver, the *E.A. Rawling,* the previous year. The ship was seized, however, by Federal authorities on the suspicion of being a slaver. Not to be deterred, Lamar persisted in spite of pressure and disapproval from family and friends.

In Brunswick, the *Wanderer* was quickly outfitted for its illegal mission with special cargo binds for holding human captives. Next, a captain and crew were chosen. Under cover of night, she slipped out to sea. Her destination: the West Coast of Africa.

After anchoring at the mouth of the Congo River—laden with merchandise to be traded for slaves—Lamar sent a small shore party to meet with tribal chief King Dahominey.

Negotiations were quick and a deal was made: 750 males between the ages of thirteen and eighteen were to be delivered at the price of $1 to $3 per head. The captives, naked and bloody from a forced march through the jungle, soon arrived. Most of them had been kidnapped by competing tribes.

On her return voyage, the *Wanderer* eluded both American and English navies patrolling the African coast in search of slavers. Within a few weeks she was back in American waters. While the *Wanderer* slipped past the U.S. fort guarding the approaches to Brunswick, Lamar threw a party for the fort's officers and men, keeping them occupied.

About 100 slaves were loaded on boats and sent up the Savannah River while the balance went ashore and were handed over to two old field hands, also originally from Africa. From the field hands the captives soon learned their sad fate.

On the open market, most of the slaves brought anywhere from $500 to $700 apiece, an amazing profit for their captors.

FATEFUL VOYAGE

That same year the *Wanderer* again set sail for the African coast. Again, a deal was made with tribal chiefs and again unfortunate captives were brought to America, this time landing on Jekyll Island. Lamar, true to form, was found dining and wining the officers and men in the coastal fort as his ship slipped by unseen.

But unlike the earlier voyage, word spread quickly and newspapers in Washington, D.C., Boston, and New York carried reports of the ship's actions.

On December 8, U.S. Attorney Joseph Ganahl of Savannah was officially notified of the *Wanderer's* actions. A week before Christmas about forty witnesses were called to give depositions, and the revenue cutter *James C. Dobbins* steamed to Brunswick to seize Lamar's ship. Law enforcement officials also tried to secure some of the slaves brought over on the ship but without success. They had all been either hidden or transported out of the area.

The *Wanderer's* books, charts, and logs were confiscated. Finally, a young boy who had been taken captive and brought over on the slaver was taken into custody. But within a few days he mysteriously disappeared. He was not seen again.

Depositions proved that the *Wanderer* did, in fact, illegally engage in the slave trade. The ship's title was transferred to the federal government and put for sale at public auction at the U.S. Customs House on Bay Street in Savannah. After a long and intense period of bidding, the ship went to the highest bidder— Charles Lamar.

A number of trials were convened against the ship's owners and crew. But justice would not have her day. Through legal maneuvering, most of the cases were held over until the April 1860 court session.

When the court did convene, three members facing piracy charges in connection with the *Wanderer* were acquitted. In a separate trial the same jury also acquitted another member of the crew.

The case became so controversial, heightening the slavery debate, that many believed it hastened the start of the Civil War. And it was the threat of war between North and South that placed the other *Wanderer* cases on hold.

By 1861, the *Wanderer* was forgotten and relegated to the annals of American history.

After hostilities began, the *Wanderer* was briefly used by the Confederate government. But she was captured by Union forces at Key West in 1861 and converted to a revenue cutter.

After the war, the ship was used in the coconut trade, sailing between the islands off the Honduran coast and the United States. She ran aground on January 27, 1871, at Cape Muisi on the east coast of Cuba. Her hull and remains were visible for years until wind, weather, and breaking waves finally pounded her into oblivion, ending an ugly chapter in American history.

— ∞ —

Bobby Jones Plays Savannah

After taking the entire winter off from golf, Robert Tyre "Bobby" Jones blew into Savannah on a whirlwind. Scheduled to play in the 1930 Savannah Open at the Savannah Golf Club on President Street, the twenty-eight-year-year-old Atlanta attorney had already proven himself to be the premier golfer of his era. He won the 1923, 1926, and 1929 U.S. Opens, was a four-time U.S. national amateur champion, and in 1926 became the first player to win both the U.S. and British Opens. In 1930, he would etch his name forever in the annals of sports greatness.

THE SAVANNAH OPEN

With the swing of a club, the Savannah Open was officially kicked off on Thursday, February 20, 1930. The first day belonged to Jones. Only days after leaving his law practice and with only one practice round under his belt, he was hotter than ever. He shaved seven strokes off par, recording nine birdies and an eagle, shooting a 67, a new club record.

But his competition lay in wait. Twenty-one-year-old Horton Smith came out Friday morning determined to make his own history, matching Jones stroke for stroke, shattering the one-day-old record with a 66. Jones shot a dismal 75 that day, taking 7 strokes at the somewhat easy second hole. The next day American sportswriters called it "the ugly 7."

Not to be outdone, Jones bounced back and reclaimed the club record on Saturday with a brilliant performance, shooting a 65. His score going out was 33; coming home he carded a 32. Except for a couple of putting slips, he would have scored in the low 60s. With the tournament prize in sight, Jones wavered on the final round, shooting two under par for a score of 72.

Smith continued his par-shattering play through the final two rounds of the tournament on Saturday. He hit 10 birdies as he drove, putted, and chipped his way across the final 36 holes. Smith's scorecard at the end of the tournament showed 278 for 72 holes. Jones hit 279 for 72 holes. Defeating Jones by a single stroke, Smith claimed the championship and the $1,000 purse.

Bobby Jones during his Grand Slam year. (Photo from the
author's collection)

Seven strokes behind Smith was the Scotch pro, Bobby
Cruickshunk, who won $500, shooting a 69 on the final round. J.
Fairly Clark of Savannah shot two superb rounds with a 68 and 69,
but blew it on the final 36 holes and ended up in a three-way tie for
fifth place.

On February 23, one local sports page read: "Horton Smith

Beats Bobby Jones by a Stroke: Smith shoots a 70 and 71 to top the field and takes the $1,000 prize. Bobby Jones falters after breaking the club record." It would be the last formal competition that Jones would ever lose.

The *New York Times* covered the story, showing photos of both Smith and Jones.

As if prophetic, a sportswriter wrote, "This may be the year in which Robert will establish a record that will stand until the day golf no longer will be played in this sphere." No truer words have ever flowed from the pen of a sportswriter.

THE GRAND SLAM OF GOLF

After the Savannah Open, Jones was unstoppable, winning first the British Open, then the British Amateur Open. Halfway to the heralded and unprecedented Grand Slam of golf, Jones was honored with a ticker tape parade through the streets of New York.

Jones completed the sweep, taking the U.S. Open and the U.S. Amateur Open, winning the Grand Slam of golf. Today's Grand Slam consists of the U.S. Open, the Master's, the British Open, and the PGA.

Only two months after attaining the pinnacle of the golfing world, Jones officially retired from the game. He was only twenty-eight. He founded the Master's tournament, however, in 1934 and re-emerged from retirement once a year to play in the prestigious event.

In what has been described as the golden age of sports, Jones stood shoulder to shoulder with other sports legends, Babe Ruth, Jack Dempsey, and Red Grange, defining and shaping the game into what it is today. Playing only three months out of every year, Jones won thirteen national championships in an eight-year run—becoming an almost mythic figure. While his driver and putter were his best weapons, it was Jones' will to win that put him in a class by himself.

Off the course, Jones designed golf clubs, wrote four books, including *Bobby Jones on Golf,* wrote a series of twice-weekly columns from 1927 to 1935, and gave instructional performances in several motion pictures, in addition to a running a full-time law practice.

Even with the emergence of new golf superstars such as Arnold Palmer and Jack Nicklaus in the 1960s, and later Tiger Woods, Jones' Grand Slam achievement stands alone to this day.

Stricken with syringomyelia, a spinal disease, Jones became confined to a wheelchair in 1958 and subsequently died in 1971.

The words of Freddie McLeod, a golf pro at Columbia Country Club during the 1930s, serve as a lasting tribute to Jones' brilliance and level of play.

"There are so few faults in Jones' swing," McLeod said at the time, "that after a layoff from the game he has nothing to guard against when he resumes play. Jones' swing is faultlessly smooth and he has marvelous judgment of distance, and his putting touch never seems to forsake him. You can not compare him to any one else."

Savannah Hosts
International Road Races

With fans cheering wildly and stock cars revving their engines, the checkered flag was finally lowered. As the cars gained speed and headed down Victory Drive, racing history was being made. Thus began the great Savannah road races of 1908-1911.

It was no easy task getting the races to Savannah, however. Beginning in 1900, the coveted Vanderbilt Cup, the premier racing event, was held on Long Island, New York. But by 1907 problems had developed. Residents disapproved of the course running through their neighborhoods, and to complicate matters, spectators got on the track during races, endangering both themselves and the drivers. Many were injured and some died. Long Island decided to postpone the races for at least a year.

When word reached Savannah that the races were up for grabs, Savannah Automobile Club president Frank Beatty sprung to action. Without having a track to race on, he announced March 18 and 19, 1908, as the dates for the Savannah races.

Beatty lobbied both race promoters and national organizations, trying to persuade them to choose Savannah as the site of the next Vanderbilt Cup. Not only did Savannah provide safer racing conditions than Long Island, Beatty claimed, but the city could offer a superior track.

With help from city and county governments, a track was soon in progress. Beatty allowed nothing to interfere with the making of the course. Cuts were made through lawns, curves were banked (some which still stand today), bridges were spanned, and dirt roads were covered with gravel and sand. Finally, oil was spread over the course to reduce dust. A well-oiled road could remain virtually dust free for up to a year.

THE TRACK

By the time it was completed, the track covered nearly 20 miles. It started at the grandstand on Estill Avenue (now Victory Drive) and stretched to Bull Street. From Bull Street it ran to White Bluff Road, then headed east onto Montgomery Cross Road. Following Montgomery, it headed northeast to Ferguson Avenue, then to a stretch of Skidaway Road, through Isle of Hope, through Thunderbolt, and finally back to Estill Avenue.

THE RACES BEGIN

Two events were scheduled for opening day, March 18—the Southern Runabout Cup Race, a 176-mile run, and the Southern High Powered Cup Race. The next day, the Savannah Challenge Cup was held. It covered twenty laps for a total of 360 miles.

The Savannah Challenge Cup provided a thrilling race, with cars changing the lead several times during the first ten laps. Receiving both national and international press coverage, the road races were deemed a success.

In November, races were also held. The first race, the Grand Prize of the Automobile Club of America, was won by Louis Wagner in a Fiat. His average speed was 65 m.p.h. The Grand Prize race was truly international, with six entries from France, six from Italy, three from Germany, and six from the United States.

Despite the success in Savannah, a decision was made to return the races to Long Island the next year. But Savannah racing enthusiasts lobbied to bring them back.

On November 11, 1910, Savannah hosted two races. The following day it hosted the Grand Prize Cup. With speeds exceeding 75 m.p.h., cars were getting faster and more sophisticated. Soon racing would change forever. But before it did, Savannah had one more year to enjoy the sport.

Three races—the Tiedeman Trophy, the Savannah Challenge Cup, and the Vanderbilt Cup—were held in Savannah on November 27, 1911. On November 30, the Grand Prize Cup was held.

The morning of the 30th was particularly cold. In fact, it was so brisk that whiskey was served in the grandstands and nobody complained.

As it became more and more difficult to keep people off the track, the military was called in to help stand guard. But it wouldn't be enough, at least for one unfortunate driver.

Jay McNay was instantly killed when he lost control of his car trying to avoid a cart that had ventured across his path on LaRoche Avenue. Despite this misfortune, the races remained popular.

But the success of the races also led to their demise. They heightened the automobile frenzy and soon Savannahians were seen whizzing around town. And the roads were of such quality that it provided Savannahians easy access to the city's outskirts. Soon, Savannah's first suburbs went up, many along the path of the racing track.

Savannah could no longer host a race without relocating the track a great distance from the city. Savannah hosted its last international racing event in 1911.

It would be a quarter century before racing enthusiasts tried again to attract major racing to Savannah. Even with a new track on Hutchinson Island, it proved a fruitless cause. Savannah's glory days of racing were long behind her.

Tracing Pulaski's Footsteps

After nearly five years and $1 million, the Pulaski monument finally returned to Monterey Square. Yet, DNA evidence proving that the remains buried there are Casimir Pulaski's is still inconclusive. While citizens wait, Savannah still pays homage to the fallen hero.

Yet, Pulaski's service for the cause of liberty is not limited just to the Savannah area. To fully appreciate the young general is to follow his footsteps, from his native Poland, to France, to his arrival and subsequent fighting in America. With his untimely death, he became both a national and international figure.

Monuments erected in his honor stand in Chicago, South Bend, Indiana, and Poland as well as Savannah. Every October 1, New York City honors Pulaski with its Pulaski Day Parade. In Illinois, the first Monday in March is celebrated yearly as Pulaski Day. And in his native Poland he is revered as a national hero.

Born in Poland in 1747 to wealthy parents, Casimir Pulaski left for France in 1768 to study law. While there, he also received military training. But Poland was coming apart at the seams, suffering political revolt. Pulaski returned home and fought with the Confederation of Bar, a patriotic Polish uprising against Russian control of Poland and its puppet leader, Polish King Stanislaus Augustus.

Yet, things soon soured for Pulaski. He was implicated in a plot to kill Augustus and sentenced to prison. After his release, he fled Poland, first heading to Turkey and then to France. While in Paris, the young Pole met American ambassador Benjamin Franklin, became intrigued with the ideals of the American struggle for independence, and applied for a commission in the newly formed Continental army.

With a letter of recommendation and a personal endorsement from Franklin, Pulaski presented himself to the Continental Congress in March 1777.

BRANDYWINE AND TRENTON

Waiting for a command to materialize, Pulaski joined George Washington's staff and was at the battle of Brandywine Creek, positioned toward the rear of the battle with the general and his staff. Yet, the day turned out badly for the American army as their columns began to crumble under the withering fire of a more disciplined, better-equipped British army.

As the Continentals floundered on the field, the British were preparing to seal Washington's only route of escape. Eager to prove himself, Pulaski asked for command of Washington's bodyguard. Within pistol shot of the Redcoats, the young Pole launched a counterattack with about thirty mounted soldiers, buying time and allowing Washington's forces to retreat, thus preventing military disaster.

Four days later, with Washington's blessing, Congress rewarded Pulaski with the rank of brigadier general and placed him in command of four horse regiments, the largest cavalry command in the American army.

In his letter to Congress, Washington wrote,

> This gentleman has been, like us, engaged in defending the liberty and independence of his country and sacrificed his fortune to his zeal for these objects. He derives from hence a title to our respect that ought to operate in his favor as far as the good of the services will permit.

After Brandywine, Pulaski served conspicuously in fighting at both Warren Tavern, near Philadelphia, and at Germantown.

Pulaski's troops wintered in Trenton and took part in the operations of Gen. "Mad Anthony" Wayne. While foraging for supplies near Huddonfield, New Jersey, Pulaski and a small squad were surprised by a division of British regulars. During the skirmish, Pulaski's mount was shot from under him, but he continued in hand to hand combat, eventually capturing several British soldiers. As a result he was assigned to special duty at Valley Forge, once again becoming a favorite of General Washington.

INDEPENDENT COMMAND

In an effort to turn his cavalry corps into a more mobile fighting force, Pulaski requested permission to revise cavalry tactics. Not only did the American high command disagree with his modifications, but he also clashed with one of his superiors, General Wayne.

Appealing to Congress for more cavalry, Pulaski was again denied. He tendered his resignation in frustration. But Congress soon authorized Pulaski to raise an independent command of lancers and light infantry. Setting up headquarters in Baltimore, Pulaski spent an estimated $50,000 of his own funds purchasing high-grade horses and outfitting them for battle. His force became truly international. Poles, Frenchmen, Americans, Irish, and Germans joined its ranks, creating the soon heralded Pulaski Legion.

The Pulaski Legion became the training ground for American cavalry officers, including "Light Horse" Harry Lee, Robert E. Lee's father. The best compliment paid to the Pulaski Legion came from the lips of a British officer who called them "simply the best damn cavalry the rebels ever had."

The Pulaski Legion fought at Egg Harbor, New Jersey, on October 15, 1778, and later at Osborne's Island, crushing their British counterparts. After spending most of the winter of 1778 in New Jersey, Pulaski was ordered to South Carolina to assist Gen. Benjamin Lincoln in his struggle to hold Charleston.

Arriving on May 8, 1779, the Pulaski Legion lived up to their reputation, tipping the balance of the struggle for Charleston to the Continental Army. As a result, British momentum in the Southern states stalled, and American morale was boosted. But the most crucial test was in Savannah, 100 miles away, under British occupation and heavily fortified. Lincoln planned to take the city at all costs. It would be Lincoln's as well as Pulaski's toughest military challenge.

Trying to follow up on his success at Charleston, Lincoln devised a plan to rescue Savannah from British occupation. Yet, this was no Charleston. Facing him were heavily entrenched British army regulars and regiments of South Carolina Tories.

Lincoln's plan was two-fold. His forces would lay siege to Savannah by land while forty French warships, under the command of Count Charles-Henri d'Estaing, would cannonade the city by sea. Militarily sound, the combined land and sea assault would have worked if executed as planned.

On September 12, 1779, 3,500 French troops, including Irish enlistees and black Haitian volunteers, landed at Beaulieu's Plantation on the Vernonburg River, about 12 miles south of

Savannah, and proceeded northward. A combined army of 1,500 Continentals and local militiamen united with d'Estaing's forces on the 16th and began to carry out operations.

As the Allied columns approached town, Lincoln and d'Estaing demanded its surrender. Gen. Augustin Provost, commander of British fortifications, however, requested twenty-four hours to think over his decision. As twenty-four hours passed, Provost shrewdly seized the day, calling up 800 additional troops from the South Carolina coast. The next morning Provost sent word to Lincoln and d'Estaing declining to surrender.

Riding ahead of the advancing columns on reconnaissance, the Pulaski Legion began testing British outposts, driving several back and clearing a path for the Allied army to advance. Finally, on October 4, Allied cannon lay siege to the city, but with little effect.

Casting an anxious eye toward his fleet, d'Estaing feared that a prolonged siege would put his ships in jeopardy. He quickly changed battle plans. Savannah would be taken by storm, an all-out land assault. Though Lincoln disagreed, he capitulated, forced to appease his French counterpart.

A DOOMED ATTACK

Early dawn, October 9, 1779, on the western outskirts of Savannah: Under cover of darkness, blue-clad Continental Army regulars begin the attack. Their objective is straightforward: to breach Spring Hill Redoubt, the strongest point in British fortifications. Across the battlefield to their right, three French columns, nearly 3,000 men strong, wait for word to advance. The Pulaski Legion remains in the rear with orders to follow behind the French columns.

But the attack is doomed from the start; deceit and betrayal crush any Allied hopes of victory. The night before, Sgt. Major James Curry of Charleston slipped past Continental sentries and deserted to British lines, informing them of Allied battle plans.

While American and French troops slept, the British quietly shifted men and munitions to meet what was to be a predawn surprise attack.

As the first Continental troops approach, British cannon open up, cutting the troops to pieces. With marked discipline, the troops close ranks and press the assault.

Led by d'Estaing, French troops begin marching toward the British breastworks from the east, but are also met by sheets of musketry and cannon fire. After a period of intense fighting, Allied forces push back resistance and plant the colors on the British parapets near Spring Hill Redoubt. But the victory is fleeting.

The second French column hesitates, lost in the dark, caught in mud and swamp. Soon, Allied troops begin to flounder and fall back. Pulaski, seeing the advance crumble, makes a bold, even reckless dash, leading 200 horsemen toward the breastworks. But to no avail. Flesh and blood wither under a barrage of artillery and musket balls.

Pulaski, struck in the groin by a piece of grapeshot, drops from his mount. His fall halts the advance, and his squadron retreats. Paul Bentalon of Baltimore, one of Pulaski's captains, rushes the general off the battlefield.

Casualties that day were horrific. Of an attacking force of around 4,000, the Allies suffer over 800 casualties—244 killed, 584 wounded. British casualties were light, only 40 killed and 63 wounded.

Many historians claim that the most desperate battle of the Revolution was fought at the British fortifications in Savannah. The battlefield covered a relatively small area, from a point just south of Liberty Street to Oglethorpe Avenue to the north.

Pulaski's death was regarded as a national catastrophe. One month after the general's death George Washington issued an order for the day to troops under his command: on November 11, the password "Pulaski" was to be used, followed by "Poland" as the response.

Count d'Estaing, twice wounded, lived, though his pride and reputation did not. A few years later, however, during the French Revolution, he died at the guillotine. Adding insult to injury, a British expedition seized Charleston in May 1780.

CONFLICTING THEORIES

Two versions of Pulaski's death emerged soon after the battle. Both agree that Pulaski was wounded during the unsuccessful Siege of Savannah on October 9, 1779, and died two days later.

The first theory claims that the fallen hero was taken off the field and transported to the *Wasp,* an Allied brig. With Pulaski on board, the *Wasp* was to have taken the general to Charleston. En route to Charleston, this account claims, Pulaski died and was subsequently buried at sea.

According to Dr. Joseph Johnson, a surgeon who claimed to have removed Pulaski's leg in an effort to save the general's life, Pulaski was buried on land. Later, however, adding to the confusion, Johnson changed his story and claimed that Pulaski died on the trip to Charleston and was buried at sea.

But others vehemently disagree. They claim that Pulaski was carried to Greenwich Plantation, near Thunderbolt, where he died surrounded by a group of his officers. By torchlight, they purport, his comrades buried the general in a grave on the plantation. Later, he was re-interred beneath his monument at Monterey Square.

Whether Pulaski's body was consigned to a watery grave or placed beneath the Georgia sod may be of little consequence. For, Casimir Pulaski, once young, brave, and daring, did indeed fall in Savannah for the cause of liberty, something that no amount of DNA evidence or lack thereof can change.

The Savannah Theater

Surviving nearly two centuries, with changes of ownership, numerous fires, and as many remodelings, the Savannah Theater has the distinction of being the oldest playhouse in continuous operation in the United States. The great names of 18th-century drama played there, and its history has paralleled that of Savannah and the nation. In 2018 the theater will celebrate its 200th anniversary.

SAVANNAH'S FIRST THEATER

Soon after British troops evacuated Savannah during the Revolutionary War, the city opened a theater on Franklin Square.

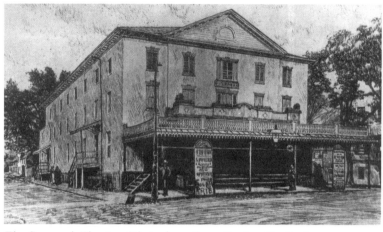

The Savannah Theater. (Photo from the author's collection)

The theater was too small, however, and Savannahians demanded a new one.

In 1810, efforts were begun to provide for a new playhouse. After a few thousand dollars had been raised, the project was scrapped because of the troubles leading to the War of 1812. With the close of the war in 1815, the resumption of commerce, and connections with affluent customers abroad, Savannah ascended to new heights of economic prosperity.

To rival neighboring Charleston, Savannahians once again lobbied for a new theater. Charleston had already been operating two theaters since the 1790s and Savannah determined to outdo its closest neighbor, or at least to try.

With the theater movement gaining momentum in 1816, the state legislature granted a charter calling into existence the Stockholders of the Savannah Theater Corporation. Following the state's lead, the city granted the vacant lots fronting Bull Street and Chippewa Square, and William Jay, in town less than a year, was hired as architect. It was completed in only nine months, and the grand opening was scheduled for December.

OPENING NIGHT

On the evening of December 4, 1818, the Savannah Theater

opened with a double billing: Andrew Cherry's comedy, "The Soldier's Daughter," and the farce "Raising the Wind." The newspapers ran the following announcement:

> Admission to boxes and to the pit, $1; to the gallery, 50 cents. Smoking in the theater cannot be allowed. The doors to be opened half past five and the performance to commence at half past 6 o'clock precisely.

Crowds poured into the theater on opening night, eagerly greeting the first performers. Yet all weren't so happy. Many complained that most women's hair was piled so high that they were blocked from seeing the performance. True to form, most fashionable ladies didn't pay attention to the gentlemen's pleas. Commenting on the complaint, the *Georgian* ran the following headline the next morning: "[headdress] might be mistaken for the steeple of the new brick church . . ."

Yet, ladies' hairstyles weren't the only complaints. That night, in the galleries above the main seats, the sound of cracking nuts was heard. Many claimed that the cheap seats, only 50 cents, attracted the wrong crowd. No matter, the cracking of nuts continued and ladies' hair stayed high—despite protests and cries of outrage.

The theater was a marvel to behold. Originally seating 1,000 spectators, it boasted two rows of boxes supported by sixteen cast-iron, fluted columns with gilt capitals and bases. The panels of the lower boxes were adorned with golden eagles, with wreathes of green foliage set against a white background. Between the boxes was a pilaster panel, laid on crimson and enriched with gold on a scroll. The second tier of boxes was ornamented with basso-relievos. The upper circle was relieved by a lyre and a wreath, the first in green and the second in gold on white panels.

The upper circle, where the disconcerting sound of cracking nuts was reported, was open to the lobbies, and the stage doors and boxes were paneled with gold mountings. The arch above the proscenium of the stage was decorated with green and gold. The seats in the boxes were covered with crimson cloth; those in the pit were green. An allegorical scene was painted on the ceiling. The drop curtain, elaborately painted, was shipped in from New York. The structure's exterior was made with Savannah Grey Brick.

Since that colorful opening night, the theater has stood the ravages of time. As soon as the first theatrical season came to a close on April 5, turbulent times hit again as the nation experienced bank panic. And, in 1820, Savannah suffered one of many devastating fires that destroyed much of the city. Later the same year the dreaded Black Vomit—yellow fever—claimed thousands, closing down the city for months. Yet despite the odds the theater continued to flourish.

EVIL LURKING IN THE SHADOWS

It is possible that Abraham Lincoln's assassin, John Wilkes Booth, played at the Savannah Theater in the 1850s. He traveled with his brother, noted actor Edwin Booth, to Augusta and some claim he accompanied him to Savannah for a performance.

In 1894, the theater underwent its first major alteration. It was then sold to the American Theatrical Exchange and renamed the Savannah Opera House.

The theater made national headlines in 1906 when it burned to the ground. According to period newspaper reports, the Ku Klux Klan may have started the blaze. Several nights before the fire, Thomas Dixon's play "The Clansman" was scheduled to perform. Every contemporary account suggests that the fire, which put the playhouse of out of business until it was rebuilt later that year, was the work of arsonists. "The Clansman" was moved to Thunderbolt, where it played despite claims that members of the KKK tried to halt production of the play there as well by intercepting patrons on their way to the theater.

In the early 1920s, Albert Weis bought the Savannah Theater. His son, Fred G. Weis, later opened a chain of movie theaters in Savannah and throughout the South. In 1944 and again in 1948, the theater caught fire, and both times had to be rebuilt. Yet, enough of the original structure remained to continue its claim as the country's oldest theater.

The Odyssey of
Savannah's Confederate Monument

In the middle of Forsyth Park in Savannah stands a bronze Confederate soldier atop a 40-foot base, dedicated to the memory of the Southern men and boys slain in the Civil War. For more than a century he has stood peacefully, gazing north toward his enemies. However, the origins of the monument were anything but peaceful.

In 1869, just four years after the end of the Civil War, word spread throughout the South that Confederate soldiers killed and buried at Gettysburg would have to be moved. Subsequently, Southern states made preparations to bring their war dead back home. The bodies of Georgians killed at Gettysburg were moved to what is now called Gettysburg Row in Laurel Grove Cemetery in Savannah.

The federal government's decision, however, heated passions in the South and gave rise to a movement to memorialize the Confederate dead.

In Savannah, the idea to build a grand memorial to honor the Confederate soldier gained momentum. And the Ladies Memorial Association, through cake, pie, and cookie sales and countless other charitable projects, raised nearly $25,000, an impressive sum in the ravaged postwar Southern economy.

Laden with funds, the ladies turned their energies to securing materials and a sculptor for the monument.

YANKEES NEED NOT APPLY

Three stipulations, however, would have to be met. The stone for the monument's base could not come from a Northern quarry, the sculptor could not be a "Yankee," and the monument must not cross over enemy (Northern) soil.

Though Vermont had an established marble and granite trade and was a source of inexpensive materials, it was out of the question. The ladies looked to Canada for help. They opted for sandstone from Nova Scotia, although it was less durable and more expensive, and chose Robert Reed of Canada, a Welshman by birth, to design and sculpt the statue.

Leaving the design up to Reed, the ladies' only instructions were to sculpt a life-size figure worthy of the honor and respect due the common Confederate soldier.

By the fall of 1874 the monument was ready for shipment. To keep it from passing over or touching Northern soil, a British schooner, the *Mary Louise,* was contracted to transport the materials from Canada. The captain, however, made one fatal mistake that would prove problematic. He forgot to submit the required manifests of his cargo to federal authorities.

To cheers and applause, the *Mary Louise* sailed into Savannah on Christmas Day 1874. But the excitement soon turned sour. U.S. customs agents, representing the then-hated Yankee government, confiscated the ship's cargo, threatening to sell the contents at auction. But Col. James Atkins, Savannah collector of customs, fearing reprisals from the indignant ladies, came to the rescue. He expedited the process, collecting $1,100 duty fees imposed on the foreign vessel, and quickly turned the material over to the consignees.

The materials made their way from the ship to Forsyth Park, where they were assembled. The following May a dedication and memorial service was held and the monument unveiled.

On the top pedestal of the monument stood the life-size likeness of a woman in a flowing robe named "Silence." In the opening below was a life-size statue named "Judgment."

On the monument's base are pilasters with patriotic mottos. The north panel depicts a figure of a prostrate woman representing the South in mourning. From her left side she lets a branch of laurel fall. In another corner is a group of weeping willows. On each corner there are cherubs. The two sides of the lateral panels bear inscriptions.

One panel bears words from the Old Testament book of Ezekiel: "Come from the four winds oh breath, And breathe upon these slain that they may live." The opposite side reads: "To the Confederate Dead, 1861-1865."

ONE MORE TRY

Though Savannahians were pleased with their accomplishment, it didn't take long before murmuring was heard. Many felt that the new statue was too ornate and didn't properly represent the ordinary soldier who had struggled in the field. The Ladies Association again turned to the drawing board, but without sufficient funds could do little.

A Mr. Wymberly DeRenne intervened and donated the necessary money to begin the process of securing a new figure to adorn the top of the monument. David Richards was chosen to carve a new sculpture, the likeness of the common Confederate infantryman. He worked using photos of Savannah veteran A.S. Bacon, who had served the entire four years of the war in the Confederate army.

A photo of Bacon, taken in the field, shows a worn hat full of holes and a ragged, weathered coat. On the coat are buttons bearing the insignias of Georgia, South Carolina, Louisiana, Alabama, Virginia, Texas, Mississippi, and Kentucky as well as two Confederate buttons. His pants had been issued during the last year of the war by the Georgia Relief and Hospital Association and were scorched at the bottom and fastened by pegs instead of a buckle. The rifle and accoutrements were also well worn from use in the field.

Unveiled in 1879, the new statue met with great enthusiasm. "Silence" was removed to watch over the Confederate dead at Gettysburg Row in Laurel Grove Cemetery. And "Judgment" was sent to Thomasville to be used as that town's war memorial. Years later, it was claimed by some that the photo of the soldier used as a model had not been Bacon, but was Hamilton M. Branch, a Confederate captain.

Yet, the story of Savannah's Confederate monument did not end in 1879. Though the first statue never crossed Northern soil, it was later learned that the current statue had Yankee written all over it. The bronze sculpture had not only traveled across Northern soil on its way to Savannah, but had also been crafted by Yankee hands.

Lillian Bragg, in her 1957 book *Old Savannah Iron Work,* explains:

> Like an O. Henry story, this little tale too has a surprise ending. Although the original monument honoring the Confederate dead was made, according to the wishes of the ladies, by a Canadian, and of Canadian marble, and it did not touch enemy ground on its trek to Savannah, the statue that took its place was cast in New York, came by railroad, thus passing over much enemy ground, and - worse luck! - was made by a Northern sculptor.

Corruption Savannah Style

Malberry Smith stepped into the garage, an odd place to cast a vote. He was new to Savannah and this was his first taste of Savannah politics. When he tried to cast his vote, he was in for the shock of his life.

"They told me that I had already voted," Smith said of that day in 1940. "Some one had voted for me. A carload of prostitutes from Charleston had been paid off and driven to the garage to vote."

An isolated incident? Hardly. This was Savannah and that was the way things were done. Politics in Savannah in the 1930s, 1940s, and 1950s were colorful and read like a work of fiction. But more than just colorful, they were filled with vote tampering, gambling, bootlegging, and every other vice imaginable. And it was better than fiction; it was the truth.

Savannah was in the throes of bossism, not unlike the political machines that controlled New York, Chicago, and Kansas City. Stories of ballot stuffing and election rigging abound.

Smith, now a retired attorney, remembers those days.

"Garages were usually the only places polling was held," he said. "They provided convenient places to control the paper ballots. Often the poll workers simply destroyed ballots or remarked them after the polls had closed."

George Oliver, Smith's former law partner and now a senior judge, recalls another favorite practice: voting from the grave.

"When someone died, his name wasn't taken off the voter's registration list," Oliver said. "During an election, if a certain number of votes were needed to insure victory, the poll workers simply used the names of the dead."

It was said at this time, perhaps accurately, that there were more registered voters at Bonaventure Cemetery than anywhere else in Savannah.

How did it ever get to that point? The answer provides an engaging story. According to Malcom Maclean, attorney and former Savannah mayor (1960-1966), the political climate in Savannah developed shortly after Northern occupation troops left the city.

"Not long after the Civil War, the law firm of Osborne and Lawrence [father of Judge Lawrence, Federal judge] developed a power base in the city," Maclean said. "It wasn't difficult to do. Voter turn out was low, and the establishment got people jobs with the city or county government, and the political machine began to manage the ballot boxes during the elections."

THE POLITICAL BOSS

Fast forward several decades and a young attorney, John Bouhan (1881-1971), appeared on the scene. From an Irish-Catholic family, Bouhan seemed destined for politics. Archie Whitefield, a retired reporter for the *Savannah Morning News,* remembers Bouhan vividly.

"He was charming, educated, and polished," Whitefield said, "also a devout churchman. He had a nice face, like someone you could trust."

Bouhan joined the law firm of Osborne and Lawrence and rose through the ranks. In time, senior partners died off and Bouhan assumed control. Later he opened his own law firm.

Though Bouhan was never officially elected to public office, his political aspirations soared and he received an appointment as the county attorney. In turn, he appointed his own handpicked men to key positions to do his bidding for him.

Said Tom Coffey, former *Savannah Morning News* reporter and editor, "Bouhan didn't control every official, but he manipulated enough to have his influence felt whenever needed. His political machine gained control of city hall, the county commission, and Chatham County's state delegates."

Boss Bouhan sat enthroned atop the political hierarchy, and both Savannah and Chatham County were his footstools. Mayors, aldermen, county commissioners, and state representatives all beckoned when Boss Bouhan called.

"Not since occupation had the city witnessed such subjugation," Maclean said.

Frank W. "Sonny" Seiler, an attorney at Bouhan's law firm, remembers Bouhan fondly. "Bouhan was a good politician, and he always had a smile on his face," said Seiler.

Though Seiler joined the firm as a green attorney in 1960 (toward the end of Bouhan's political reign) and had no dealings in politics, he did have his ear to the wall and kept abreast of the political scene in Savannah.

"One of Bouhan's main strengths was his organization—staying in touch with people personally," Seiler said. "Those days it was worth being in politics because you could give jobs out. You were in control, could hire policemen, appoint officials.

"The crowd with the best poll workers had the advantage. They worked the neighborhoods, legally. Those days were filled with plain old hard politics."

Bouhan was also cozy with the governor's office, and the federal government, according to many, either kept its distance or seemed disinterested.

"Savannah in the early '40s was in pretty bad shape," Malberry Smith said. "Many streets were unpaved, the sanitation equipment was dilapidated and rusted. U.S. Sen. Dick Russell hadn't been in Savannah in years. All he had to do for support was call Bouhan."

One example of the workings of the political machine was the building of a bridge across the Savannah River to South Carolina. Municipal bonds were issued to help finance the project—the original Talmadge Bridge—named for Gov. Eugene Talmadge, one of Bouhan's close friends. As county attorney, Bouhan was entitled to a fee on every bond issued. According to one former newsman, Bouhan netted over $40,000 on the deal.

Where were the local police at this time? They, too, allegedly got a piece, albeit a small piece, of the action. According to Marvin Strode, a retired Savannah policeman who rose through the ranks to captain, officers were grossly underpaid and often worked second jobs to support their families. Many opted for an easier way to supplement their income. They usually received a ten- or twenty-dollar bill to look the other way.

"Not that they were corrupt, they merely saw this as part of the status quo. They needed the money," said Strode. "This was before the police department was modernized," he added. "We had eight cars in the entire police force. At times, we were lucky if we had two cars that would start."

A trustee pours out confiscated moonshine as Savannah
police watch. Reporter Tom Coffey records the event.
(Photo courtesy Marvin Strode)

Adding to the fray, during Bouhan's reign policemen were
appointed by the political machine and received little if any formal
training. Often, a young officer would be hired one day and be out
on patrol by the next day.

In addition to voting fraud and corruption, the city's other
vices—gambling, running moonshine, and prostitution—all vied
for acknowledgment as the most flagrant.

Gambling in Savannah took several forms. Many played bolitia,
a numbers game prevalent in the black community.

To play bolitia, you'd have to hook up with one of the runners
on the street. You would buy a ticket, as many as you wanted, with
a number between 1 and 99 written on it. The ticket would serve as
your receipt. At day's end, the winning number would be drawn.
But the location of the drawing would often be changed to throw
off any police with a conscience.

During the drawing, a sack filled with numbered ping pong
balls would be shaken, passed around, and shaken some more. The

bolitia operator would then retrieve one of the ping pong balls. If the number on the ball matched your ticket, you would be the winner. Payoffs varied with the amount betted. According to Strode, the best payoff would be on a $100 bet. It paid off ten to one.

However, if the payoff was too big, you might have trouble collecting the proceeds.

"Bolitia was more or less honest," said Coffey, "unless a number was played too heavily. If that happened, they had a way of making sure the number never came up."

Bolitia also had a cast of colorful characters. Two white men, Snippy Garrity and Bubba Johnson, called the shots. And Sloppy Joe Bellinger, a large black man weighing 400 pound at his death, was also a bolitia kingpin. These men in turn hired subordinates to run the show for them.

Police, reluctant to provoke the powers that be, did little about the problems, while the political machine lined its pockets with huge profits.

Slot machines were also common in those days. They could be played for only a nickel. They first became a hit at Savannah Beach (Tybee), but soon all of Savannah became infected. You could pull a lever at the Brass Rail or the Tybrisa Pavilion on Tybee Island, at Johnny Harris Restaurant on Victory Drive, at Al Remler's Club Royale on Skidaway Road, and at Barbee's Pavilion at Isle at Hope, as well as at a dozen county roadhouses.

Norman Heidt, current CEO of Johnny Harris Restaurant, worked at the restaurant as a boy.

"Red Donaldson [the owner] always had a bottle of liquor put under the seat of the health inspector as well as other officials," Heidt said. "The county sheriff, William Harris, met privately with Donaldson every week."

Slot machines in Johnny Harris Restaurant were played in a private dining room (still in use today), and poker games were held in a separate room behind the dance floor. The games would last for days, with thousands of dollars up for grabs. Games would become so intense that men would refuse to leave the gambling table.

"They ate, drifted to sleep, and some even urinated on themselves instead of breaking away from the games," recalled the wife of a former poker player.

Though against state law, state officials didn't interfere with the gambling. In exchange for their non-concern, the explanation goes, city officials didn't ask the state for funds for city roads.

Local podiatrist Bill Harris claims that the corruption wasn't so passive. He should know. He was a boy when his father, William Harris, was county sheriff (1948-1960). When asked about the roads/gambling deal between Savannah and the state, Harris balked.

"They were paid off," he said. "They received money under the table. It was a political system. You had the Irish Catholic, the Crackers or Baptists, the Jews, and the blacks. That's the way things were run, and they were run pretty damn good."

Harris defended Bouhan.

"Bouhan rose out of the Irish trying to improve their lives," he said. "Just trying to help each other out."

Frank Downing, an attorney and Thunderbolt judge, disagrees.

"My father, an Irish Catholic, years ago, in the '20s, and '30s, was a major player in the political machine," he said. "But if you raised your head, Irish or not, Bouhan would knock it off. He was in it for himself."

BO PEEP'S POOL HALL

Mention Bo Peep's today to any native Savannahian over the age of fifty and you'll likely get a smile. The pool hall was owned and operated by Wolfe "Bo Peep" Silver. Located on Drayton and Congress streets across from Christ Church, it was a longtime favorite.

Standing just five feet tall, Wolfe Silver was an intriguing man. Born into a Jewish family in London, he moved to the States with his parents when he was six.

Due to financial problems, Silver dropped out of school during the third grade. By the time he was a young man, according to grandson Murray Silver, Jr., Bo Peep was bootlegging illegal liquor across the country during Prohibition, often making a Savannah to New York run or a Savannah to New Orleans run. When Prohibition was repealed, he opened a small pool hall in Savannah and named it Bo Peep's.

By the 1930s, Bo Peep was making tons of money. An ardent defender of his grandfather, Murray rationalized, "But he also helped out churches, synagogues and people in need."

To appease neighboring Christ Church, which really didn't want a pool hall across the street, Bo Peep floated cash to the church, according to Julian Silver, Bo Peep's son.

"We had an agreement with the church," said Julian, who worked for his father. "Anything the church asked for, we did. Once, we helped put on a new roof."

By all accounts, Bo Peep's was a thriving place. By day it was a restaurant and frequented by a diverse mix of people: businessmen, attorneys, blue-collar workers, and pretty young ladies. But no lady would be caught there at night. After sunset, Bo Peep's hopped with activity.

"The liquor flowed and the numbers ran," said Murray. "You could bet on horses, baseball games, or just about anything else."

"You could do anything there, place a bet, play a game of pool, or go to the bar and get a mixed drink," recalled Coffey, who visited Bo Peep's as a young reporter.

Yet, Bo Peep kept in the middle of the road politically, financially supporting all candidates who ran for office, ensuring a steady steam of business and a steady crop of cash.

Moonshine and stills were also thriving in Savannah from the 1920s to the 1950s. Police, less tolerant of stills than gambling, often went on raids. But one former officer said that for years a still was located on Habersham Street, directly across from the police barracks.

Marvin Strode tells how police would conduct moonshine raids. At times, he said, they would enter a suspected house only to have potash thrown on them. One raid, according to Strode, was particularly humorous.

"We raided a house but couldn't find a still or even a trace of liquor," he said. "Finally we gave up. But before we left, one thirsty officer went into the kitchen for a drink of water. What came out of the faucet was not water but moonshine. The bootleggers had a hidden keg in the attic hooked up to the faucet in the kitchen."

What did average citizens think of all this at the time? According to most sources, the average Savannahian was apathetic about the whole situation. Yet, the die was about to change and the Bouhan machine would soon experience its first crack. According to Maclean, the city was in financial ruin. With bankruptcy looming, alarmed bankers refused to issue the city any more credit. Finally, they issued an ultimatum. City government was forced to undergo investigation by an outside consulting firm.

Griffin-Hagen & Associates, an internationally known consulting firm, was hired to analyze the city's finances and to report their findings. After four months of investigation, Griffin-Hagen filed a scathing report.

"In the history of examining governments and municipalities," they wrote, "Savannah is the worst we have ever seen."

Finally, it appeared that the city that had been lulled asleep was about to awaken.

THE BEGINNING OF REFORM

The Griffin-Hagen report was a dagger in the heart of the old political power base, but the politicians merely solidified their position and prepared to fight. The report recommended that the city switch from a strong mayor-alderman form of government to a council-manager form of government.

Under the mayor-alderman structure, aldermen ran for office at large rather than by district. The mayor was responsible for both setting policy and carrying it out. Under the council-manager system, the mayor and aldermen set policy and the city manager is responsible for implementing it.

The *Morning News* took up the reform cause, running an editorial suggesting that the Savannah Jaycees educate the public about the proposed form of government.

The Jaycees, made up of men mostly in their mid- to late-twenties, accepted the challenge.

Frank Cheatham, retired judge, former state delegate, and former Jaycee president, described these men.

"The majority were young World War II veterans," he said. "Because of their war experiences they were mature beyond their years. They returned home from the war and saw the conditions in Savannah and it troubled them."

The Ambucs, the League of Women Voters, and other civic organizations joined the Jaycees. Together they formed a formidable foe.

Seminars were held to help educate the public about the new form of government. Letters to both the *Morning News* and the *Evening Press,* which had different owners, were dispatched.

The *Morning News* for the most part was unsympathetic to the Bouhan machine. The *Evening Press,* however, was loyal to the Bouhan faction.

REFERENDUM

The Jaycees petitioned for a referendum to allow citizens to vote on the proposed form of government. The Bouhan machine, officially called the Chatham County Democratic Committee (CCDC), vehemently opposed the idea. Public pressure mounted, however. They conceded, and a referendum was scheduled.

"These young men were fighting an entrenched machine," recalled Cheatham, "and the public was shocked."

Finally, the stage was set.

"Things got pretty hot," recalled Joseph Tribble, former Savannah Jaycee and committee chairman.

"The summer of '51 was a classic election. The reform party gained momentum. Thousands of dollars were spent by both sides on political ads. The Rotary Club, which backed the CCDC, released the following statement: 'Savannah - the best run city in the state.'

"Everyone knew it was a farce."

According to Coffey, Bouhan tried to keep voters away from the polls.

"A large number of men—approximately 5,000—worked at Union Camp," said Coffey.

In those days, there were only two ways for the men to go home after work: the old viaduct over Bay Street, or Telfair Road. The largest shift usually knocked off around 5 in the afternoon. On election day the Bouhan machine staged an automobile accident on the west end of the viaduct—traffic was backed up for miles. Bay Street was only two lanes. Finally, someone suggested that the men take the Telfair route. They made it in time to cast their votes. Bouhan was at his end and grasping at straws.

Another tactic tried by some supporters of the Bouhan machine was to buy votes. Prostitutes and the homeless were paid a few dollars, instructed how to vote, given a registered voter's name, and driven to the polls. The Jaycees countered by following their cars, then signaling the workers inside the polls. The paid-off prostitutes and homeless were challenged and were asked the mother's maiden name of the registered voter they were trying to represent. If they couldn't give the correct answer, they were turned away.

That day the poll workers were in the thick of the action.

"We instructed poll workers: take a flash light. Don't eat or drink anything offered to you," Tribble said. "We were suspicious and thought that they would put laxatives in the drinks of the poll workers."

Voting that day was steady. After the polls closed, things heated up. Poll workers loyal to Bouhan dumped the paper ballots out on large tables. Several put pencil lead underneath their fingernails and ran them across reform ballots, disqualifying their vote. At one precinct, according to Tribble, Mrs. Barbara Maner, wife of attorney Oliver Maner, had seen enough. She sat on a box of ballots forbidding the pollsters to count them, and kept repeating, "Don't you touch me!" Soon, an election judge—a recent addition to the Savannah political scene—appeared. The ballots were counted individually to ensure accuracy.

Across town on Indian Street, things were also hot. According to Tribble, the city marshal and two hired thugs arrived and tried to instruct the pollsters how to count the votes. Again, the Jaycees responded quickly, this time with a goon squad of their own—five large men each weighing at least 250 pounds. They arrived at the Indian Street poll and the marshal and his men backed down. And finally, by days' end, the referendum had passed.

But it was only a partial victory. The next step would be even tougher—ratification in the state legislature. Chatham County had three state delegates—all loyal to Boss Bouhan. Fate, however, favored the reformers when one of the legislators, Ernest Haar, drowned in a boating accident, requiring a special election to fill his vacancy.

This provided an ideal opportunity for the reform movement to take action. Realizing they needed to be affiliated with a political party, they established the Citizen's Committee, a branch of the Democratic Party. During this period in the South, the Democratic Party was the only viable party—particularly on the local level. The Republican Party, born of Lincoln and the Civil War and identified with Reconstruction, was still political anathema in Dixie.

The Citizens Committee chose attorney Frank Cheatham to run against the CCDC's H. Saul Clark. Cheatham, only twenty-nine years old and crippled by polio since he was a boy, didn't impress Bouhan.

He slammed Cheatham, stating, "If Cheatham is elected he'll be as effective as a Pekinese dog on a coon hunt."

Cheatham, however, was no Pekinese but rather an impressive political foe. Cheatham remembered those days.

"Banks and private businesses privately contributed funds to our campaign," he said. "They were afraid to openly support us; if we lost the election, the machine would come down on them."

Cheatham beat Clark by a 2 to 1 margin. After the election, Cheatham replied, "Some Pekinese!"

The city charter was finally amended and the council-manager form of government installed, breaking the back of the Bouhan political machine.

ENFORCING THE LAWS

Former mayor Malcolm Maclean said, "The first crack in the machine—Clark beaten by Cheatham. The final blow—the installation of voting machines. Paper ballots were no longer used and votes could no longer be manipulated."

The next order of business was to clean up the city. State gambling and liquor laws began to be enforced and it looked like Savannah was on its way to complete reform. But reform was not without its casualties. Pool hall owner Bo Peep Silver got caught in the squeeze. Murray Silver, Jr., described what happened.

"My grandfather was an insider and got blasted in the cleanup. The GBI (Georgia Bureau of Investigation) accused him of several crimes and he eventually lost everything—friends, his business, money, and his respect."

With son Julian and wife Katherine in tow, Silver fled to Florida, a penniless and broken man. He committed suicide in 1963.

Another casualty of the political war was county sheriff William Harris, who, according to son Bill, was forced to crack down on businesses he had once left alone. Harris also became an unpopular man and lost the next sheriff's election. He tried his hand at the newspaper business for a while, running the *Free State,* which challenged the new political power in town. But the paper folded and the Harris family moved to Atlanta. Bill Jr. eventually enrolled in and completed medical school, returned to Savannah, and opened a medical practice.

The end for the Bouhan machine was now imminent. After losing the mayoral election, its only remaining power base was on the county commission. But by 1960, Bouhan and his political dynasty were finished, dying not with a cough but a wheeze.

Dethroned politically, Bouhan continued practicing law. He died, at the age of eighty-six, in 1971, marking the end of a political era.

Half Rubber:
The Quintessential Savannah Game

It danced. It rose, then dropped. It swerved in all kinds of erratic directions and broke just as you were swinging, often at speeds near 70 m.p.h. At times it skimmed along the grass tops, but you'd swing, usually missing and feeling a little foolish. It was half rubber—the quintessential Savannah game, born on a dozen street corners during the early 20th century.

Today a growing number of Savannahians have little knowledge of the sport, and even fewer have ever played the game. Adding insult to injury, Charleston, a neighbor and often rival to the east, now claims to be the birthplace of half rubber and may soon own a trademark to the game itself.

Originating in Savannah in the decade prior to World War I, half rubber is played with a hard rubber ball cut in half and a broom handle. It is similar to baseball, except a team consists of only three players—a pitcher, a catcher, and an outfielder. Games usually last only six or seven innings. Players rotate positions and take turns batting. Other than catching a pop fly, the only other way to retire a batter is for the catcher to snag a pitch the batter has swung at and missed. If the catcher catches a foul tip, it counts as two outs.

A hit is anything a bat's length in front of the batter. There are no doubles or triples in half rubber, only singles. You score by loading the bases and then driving in runs, one at a time. In some games a home run is any thing hit over a certain pre-set distance. And the batter remains at the plate until he is out. Good hitters have been known to torment their opponents by remaining at the plate for hours.

HALF RUBBER MEMORIES

By the 1920s, half rubber's popularity flourished and a generation of local boys came of age playing and loving the game.

"I first played in 1927 when the big boys would let me," said native Savannahian Sam Nichols, 80, now living in Fullerton, California.

"We played on 38th Street between Bull and Drayton with Jack Forehead and the two Potter boys. Occasionally, my older brother would step in with his friends and show us li'l ones how to play.

"To me half rubber is more important than *Midnight in the Garden of Good and Evil*," said Don Causey. "I've been playing the game—yes, in Savannah—since the 1950s and have been teaching my son how to play over the last few days."

ORIGINS

Not only is the birthplace of half rubber disputed, but opinions also vary on how the game developed. Some believe that a group of boys took a razor and sliced a rubber ball in half so that two games could be played instead of one. Others claim that the game developed out of financial necessity. Once the first half of the ball wore out, you could keep playing with the other half.

A 1957 *Savannah Evening Press* article offers a different version. It claims that a couple of kids were sailing soft drink bottle caps and someone picked up a stick and tried to hit one of the caps. Bottle caps bent easily, so a tennis ball was tried next, but it frayed.

Finally, a sponge rubber ball was cut in half and a new sport was born.

According to most local half-rubber enthusiasts, the sport peaked in Savannah in the 1960s. Kids perfected their skills in the streets and parks and on the beaches of the Savannah area, while adults prepared to take the game to a higher level.

"Tournaments began in the early '70s," said Charlie Russo, 58, who first played the game as a boy near his father's fish market on the corner of Waters Avenue and 31st Lane.

"Former Mayor Rousakis was instrumental in getting them going," he added, "and he gave the tournament its name—the World Invitational Halfrubber Tournament."

The Savannah tournaments were first played at Daffin Park, then moved to Grayson Stadium, and finally to Paulson Sports Complex next to Memorial Stadium.

But by the 1980s the sport began to wane, giving way in many places to its northern cousin, stickball. Today it is difficult to find a half rubber game in Savannah. The tournaments are long gone, few play it at the beach, and there seems to be little interest in reviving the sport.

The only game still being played on a consistent basis, according to Russo, takes place on Sunday afternoon at Hull Park, on 55th Street and Atlantic Avenue.

A GAME FOR SALE

A few years ago, Land Shark Productions Inc., a Charleston-based company, began selling half rubber balls and bats. Although this was not unique, they went one step further, successfully petitioning the U.S. Patent Office for an exclusive trademark to the game.

In 1998, Charleston attorney and half rubber enthusiast Paul Schwartz and Isle of Palms resident Ricky Myatt purchased Land Shark Productions' assets, including the rights to half rubber.

"Our predecessor had the trademark for the name half rubber, but let it lapse," said Schwartz. "We are currently in the process of renewing that patent."

How do you patent a sport? According to Schwartz, if approved, the trademark would prohibit other companies from marketing products under the name half rubber. But whether or not the public would have to acknowledge half rubber with a trademark symbol when using the term remains unclear. The U.S. Patent Office has not set a specific date for their conclusions.

SAVANNAH—CHARLESTON CONTROVERSY

While Charlestonians claim their city as the birthplace of half rubber, native Savannahians disagree.

"Never heard of Charleston playin' the game," said Sam Nichols. "We always thought Charlestonians only played bridge, cricket, gossip, and snooty."

Dan E. Jones, in his 1980 book *Half Rubber: The Savannah Game,* also disputes Charleston's allegations. "No one could be found in Charleston who remembered the game being played there before 1922," writes Jones, who conducted research for his book in the late 1970s.

In Savannah, however, several went on record that they played the game prior to World War I.

"Therefore," Jones concludes, "the game migrated from Savannah to Charleston, and not vice versa."

While the debate rages, it appears that neither town can fully substantiate their claims. J. Wallace Winn, a native Savannahian and principle of Oglethorpe Avenue School in the 1930s and 1940s, may have come up with the answer years ago.

"I don't believe anyone can say that they invented half rubber," he wrote. "It was an evolvement, not an invention."

West Broad Street Jazz

Music filled the streets, no matter the hour. The sound of jazz rose to the heavens and descended again—the tap, the beat, the rhythm. Crowds filled the clubs. Names such as the Cotton Club, the Hollywood Casino, the Star Theater, the Neptune Club, and the Peking Theater packed them in. Such greats as Joe "King" Oliver, Louis Armstrong, Duke Ellington, Cab Calloway, Count Basie, Chick Webb, and Ella Fitzgerald kept them coming back for more.

It was another time, another era. But this wasn't New Orleans, nor Chicago, nor even New York City—it was Savannah, and Jazz was king. And in Savannah the place to be was old West Broad Street, where the story of Jazz became a unique piece of Americana.

JAZZ CULTURE

Before Interstate 95 was constructed, before I-16 came into existence, the only route leading into Savannah was Highway 17. And Highway 17 led to West Broad Street. As a result, West Broad buzzed with activity. Not far from the north end of West Broad Street (now Martin Luther King Jr. Boulevard) was Union Station, bringing in by rail those who decided not to make the drive. Not only did West Broad have two passenger railroad stations in town, but it had two bus stations as well.

In the midst of all of this activity, West Broad Street had developed into the entrepreneurial hub of black Savannah in the decades prior to desegregation. Its heart ran from Union Station south toward Anderson Street, nearly a dozen blocks.

Lining the streets were black-owned businesses or those that catered to the black community: dry cleaners, clubs, banks, insurance companies, restaurants, churches, and the Dunbar Theater with an upstairs hotel—the only black-owned hotel in Savannah.

Entertainers, particularly vaudeville acts, began arriving around the beginning of the 1900s. By the 1920s, West Broad Street had its own distinct flavor, bringing in friends, weary travelers, and most important— jazz. The influences of these traveling musicians blended with Savannah's own unique sounds of jazz, resulting in musical magic.

"If guys were down and out, or if things were slow, they'd say 'let's go to Savannah,' because they knew something would be going on," said Teddy Adams, now sixty, director of the city's street-sweeping department and a noted jazz performer who began playing on West Broad Street when he was a junior high school student in the mid-1950s.

Social clubs would initially bring in the bands, according to Adams. In time, however, booking agents appeared, and the premier booking agent in Savannah was Frank Dilworth.

"My husband booked them all," said Louise Dilworth of her late husband. "The big names—Louis Armstrong, Ella Fitzgerald, and others. They had agencies in New York and they would contact Frank to set up gigs in Savannah."

Not only did the bands play at the clubs on West Broad Street and the small scattering of other black establishments in the area, but they also performed at the old City Auditorium near the present-day site of the Civic Center as well. But when groups played at the auditorium, according to Mrs. Dilworth, things were just heating up.

"Everybody went and had a good time," she said. "After the concert we'd go to a supper club and have dinner and soon the musicians would show up and have a jam session."

In addition to performing at West Broad Street clubs, black entertainers also played at white establishments in the area: the Tybrisa Pavilion on Tybee Island, Al Remler's Club Royale on the corner of Skidaway and Victory Drive, Johnny Harris' on Victory Drive, and others.

Though the black entertainers were welcomed at white clubs, black patrons were not.

"Blacks could always play in white clubs," said Adams, "and when they performed in black clubs, whites could go and not be bothered. But not the other way around. Blacks could not frequent the white establishments."

Jazz in Savannah, particularly West Broad Street jazz, peaked by the late 1940s and early 1950s. The city was the last leg of a circuit traveled by musicians. Some came straight from New Orleans; others made their way from New Orleans to Chicago, to Kansas City, St. Louis, New York and finally Savannah. And many of the big names wintered here as well.

Others got stranded in Savannah and decided to stay. According to Adams, noted bass player Oscar Pettiford, when only seven years old, came to Savannah with his father and stayed long enough for one of his brothers to marry.

By the mid-1950s, a group of new performers emerged as did another, different strand of jazz. Native Savannahian Stella Jackson Storms, who began singing in church as a small child, started performing professionally in 1954.

"West Broad Street was alive—very much alive," she recalled. "You could walk the street any time of the night and hear the music and see people. Some clubs had live performers, but by then others had jukeboxes. It was just a great place."

END OF AN ERA

Though West Broad bustled with activity, the 1950s would be the end of its glory days. According to Storms, other clubs sprang up and pulled people away from the area. One club, the Flamingo on Gwinett Street, brought in talent such as Ray Charles and Count Basie, adding to the problem.

Adams, however, attributes the decline of West Broad Street to desegregation.

"West Broad died mainly as a result of integration," said Adams. "By the early '60s blacks could leave the area, and in time most of the old buildings came down."

Today, a housing project stands where former clubs used to sit. The theaters are long gone, as are most of the buildings that housed other establishments from that era.

However, the music still lives and is flourishing through countless performers locally, across the country and abroad. These days, Teddy Adams, a member of the first group of inductees into the Coastal Jazz Hall of Fame, plays at various clubs on the weekends.

Stella Storms no longer performs jazz, but sings at the First Metropolitan Baptist Church on 37th Street and Jefferson, where she has been singing for fifty-six years.

And Mrs. Dilworth, still quick witted, is full of memories of a time she describes as "simply lovely."

Fire!
How Savannah Burned

S ince General Sherman decided not to raze the city during the Civil War, a misconception has developed that Savannah has been spared the torch. Nothing could be further from the truth. On five different occasions Savannah has gone up in flames, and on at least two of those occasions the city almost ceased to exist.

Though Savannah's early leaders were trained in Europe where municipal fire protection was established, for some reason they failed to include such precautions when planning the new colony of Georgia. With houses made of wood and brick ovens used for heating and cooking, early Savannah was a fire waiting to happen. And that's exactly what occurred in 1737 when the colony was just four years old.

A fire reported to have started in an oven spread quickly to nearby structures. The colonists finally extinguished it by forming a bucket brigade, but not before several homes were destroyed. The only townsman not participating, a Mr. Jones, who watched with his hands in his pockets, was arrested and jailed.

Savannah's first major fire broke out November 26, 1796. By the time the last ember was extinguished, more than 300 homes were destroyed, totaling two-thirds of the city, in an area from Bay to Oglethorpe streets, and from Barnard to Abercorn Street. At the time it was considered one of the most destructive fires in American history.

The fire began at the old City Market in Ellis Square. Once ignited, the flames spread, fed by a strong northwest wind. In the fire's path lay hundreds of wooden structures, parched due to several rainless months. By day's end hundreds of displaced citizens wandered the streets not knowing where to turn for help. In the blaze, most of the city's original structures, Oglethorpe's early Savannah, were lost. But from the ashes, Savannah rebuilt.

FIRE PROTECTION

It was no secret that Savannah had been ill prepared to deal with a substantial blaze. Many pointed fingers. Other major eastern cities—Boston, New York, and Philadelphia—had volunteer fire companies. Why didn't Savannah? According to most period accounts, the gentry, the aristocratic cotton merchants, large property owners, and tradesmen considered it beneath their dignity to participate in a volunteer fire department.

In an effort to remedy the problem, the city council appointed two fire masters and a company of twenty ax men for each city ward. Each ward was assigned a fire hook, a ladder, and rope. And all homeowners were to furnish a bucket for each fireplace in their house with a ladder of "suitable length." Savannahians hoped it would be enough.

THE FIRE OF 1820

After a lapse of twenty-four years, Savannah was once again roused by the sound of fire alarms. At 2:30 A.M. January 11, 1820, a small fire started at Mr. Boon's livery stable in the back of Mrs. Platt's boarding house on Franklin Square. As in the fire of 1796, conditions were ripe. Rain had not fallen on the city for several months and Savannah's wooden structures were little more than kindling waiting for the torch.

From Mrs. Platt's the flames spread to a neighbor's house, then to another, and soon swept along the rooftops, carried by the wind. The bright orange flames, set against the black night, would have been a spectacular sight if not for the misery and destruction they inflicted.

The fire of 1820 again gave Savannah the horrid distinction of having suffered one of the worst fires in the United States. Close to 500 structures, valued at $4 million, were lost in only eight hours. Savannah almost ceased to exist.

Nearly every structure between Broughton and Bay streets, and from Jefferson to Abercorn streets, except the State and Planters Bank and the Episcopal church, was annihilated.

Families left outside and exposed to the winter elements had few resources or places to turn for help. Soon, misery and sickness followed. A report by the *Georgian* described the situation. Families by the hundreds were "homeless, destitute, and literally naked in the streets."

Yet, relief did finally arrive. Charleston donated $10,000 and the mayor of New York City sent a check for $10,238.29, but a stipulation was attached to the New York donation. There was to be no prejudice, no distinction made on account of color in distributing the funds. The Savannah City Council, insulted that they should be considered incapable of handling their own affairs and citizens, returned the funds.

The state of Georgia contributed $35,000 in aid, $6,600 came from private donations, and the states of South Carolina, Virginia, Maryland, New York, Massachusetts, and Tennessee and the district of Maine also sent funds and provisions.

Like before, a flurry of fire prevention measures followed. New fire companies were formed and equipped. In 1821, seventy-five free men of color were allowed to form the Franklin Free Engine & Hose Company and the Union Ax & Fire Company. The city posted a reward of $5 for the first person to ring a bell to warn of fire and $3 for the second person to do so.

An act passed by the Georgia General Assembly authorized Savannah to appoint twenty-one firemen and enforce safety codes. But it was not until 1845 that fire districts were formed, engine houses built, and a respectable fire department established.

Adding insult to injury, a yellow fever epidemic also broke out in Savannah in 1820, killing thousands, until cold weather finally killed its deadly carrier—the mosquito.

As the Civil War came to a bloody conclusion, Gen. William Tecumseh Sherman and his 62,000 blue-clad devils cut a swath of destruction from the Georgia hills to the sea, the likes of which neither Georgia nor any other state had ever seen.

On December 22, 1864, the general wired President Lincoln and offered Savannah as a Christmas gift, "with 150 heavy guns and plenty of ammunition; and also about 25,000 bales of Cotton." Most Savannahians, relieved that they had not suffered the fate of much of the rest of the state, seemed to take the occupation in stride. Hopes were high that the war would finally be over by spring.

But on the evening of January 27, 1865, a fire began at the north side of Zubly Street between Ann and St. Gall. It spread quickly. The Confederate arsenal located at Broughton and West Broad streets, containing plenty of ordnance, incendiary shells, and more than fifty tons of gunpowder, lay in its path.

As the fire enveloped the arsenal, word spread and most residents fled harm's way. Within a few minutes the first shell in the arsenal exploded, then another, and what Savannah missed in the way of a military siege was now made up for.

For nearly three hours, shot, shell, and flames soared through the sky, igniting nearby structures, killing and wounding many. Some of the fragments were thrown as far as Johnson Square. The *Philadelphia,* a steamer moored at a wharf in the Savannah River, was struck by a shell fragment.

With bells sounding, panicked Savannahians fled their homes into the open, ill prepared for the freezing temperatures that greeted them, while soldiers ran around trying to help the best they could. A shell pierced the water tank atop of the reservoir tower, spilling hundreds of gallons of much needed water, which soon froze into icicles.

Able-bodied citizens labored side by side with Union soldiers to help extinguish the blaze. Before the last flame was put out more than 200 building had been destroyed.

WHO IS TO BLAME?

Despite all of the help given by Union troops, accusations surfaced. Two theories emerged. The first: Not being able to torch Savannah, many soldiers were frustrated and vented their anger by starting the fire. The second and more plausible theory places the blame on the 20th U.S. Army Corps, the unit slated to occupy the city while the balance of Sherman's troops marched on to South Carolina. Not wanting to be left behind, they supposedly started the fire in hopes of destroying the city and rejoining their comrades. Neither claim was ever substantiated.

HOGAN'S FIRE OF 1889

Poor Daniel Hogan. His name is forever associated with perhaps the worst fire Savannah has ever seen. The fire that year started at his dry goods store on the corner of Broughton and Barnard streets at seven in the morning on Halloween Day 1889.

As a clerk attempted to light a glass lantern in a show window at Hogan's store, a gust of wind blew and ignited nearby merchandise. The window was broken in an attempt to quell the fire, but to no avail. The blaze spread from the window to the second floor, sending employees scuttling to safety. Within minutes, the second floor was engulfed. At 7:15 the first of dozens of fire alarms sounded. By day's end many of the alarms would be melted by the heat.

From Hogan's store the fire leapt to an adjoining building. As his roof collapsed, a shower of sparks and embers hurled themselves into the morning sky. They found their way to virtually every rooftop on neighboring State Street. Meanwhile, according to accounts, the heat from the flames was so intense that it ignited several other buildings on Broughton and Barnard streets.

FLAMES COME TO LIFE

As fear-stricken pedestrians gazed in disbelief, flames, aided by strong gusts, turned west and ignited the Old Fellow's Hall. Sparks shot through the air, meeting newly strung electric lines, giving off an eerie pale blue light.

With the fire gaining velocity, witnesses claimed it began to make a loud, disconcerting roar. From State Street the fire headed south toward the Telfair Academy of Arts and Sciences. But this time a crew stood ready. In anticipation of the flames, the windows were covered with wet blankets and fire hoses showered the mansion with sheets of water. The only damage suffered was scorched paint and a few cracks on the exterior walls.

No one gave thought to the Independent Presbyterian Church on Bull Street. As flames were being battled elsewhere, a small cinder, about the size of a man's fist, settled in the church's tower. Within minutes it turned into a raging blaze. Within two minutes the hands of the steeple's clock ticked for the last time and then melted away from the heat.

The steeple crashed to the ground, igniting the chapel and the nearby Sunday school building. By the time the fire was under control, the church still stood, but only as a charred and smoking skeleton, a ghost of what it had once been.

ENTIRE CITY THREATENED

Sparks from the Independent Presbyterian Church ignited several other buildings in the area, sending embers airborne as far as Liberty Street toward the recently constructed DeSoto Hotel. The hotel's scaffolding caught fire several times but large crowds of determined men extinguished the small fires. After several hours, the flames had been beaten back and the hotel saved.

By three o'clock the next morning, twenty hours after the fire started, the blaze was finally under control. Though several buildings still burned and hundreds smoldered, the worst was over.

TOTAL COST

The next day, loss from the fire was estimated at $750,000. But given the enormous destruction, that early estimate seems particularly low. Unlike earlier fires, this time many had insurance. Perhaps the insurance companies had something to do with the low estimates. Savannah pledged to rebuild, and rebuild it did. Finally, it appeared that residents had learned from the past.

In 1900, a new, modern engine house was erected at the corner of Barnard and 8th streets and was equipped with an engine and combination wagon. In 1912, Savannah became the first city in the country to have a fully mechanized fire department.

Since then, the sound of fire alarms has continued to alert its citizens, rousing them at night and seizing them with fear by day. Firefighters have continued to battle blazes—but none have matched the early fires that burned Savannah.

The Rise and Fall
of the Old DeSoto Hotel

Savannah threw a gala event on New Year's Eve 1890. Not only was it a magnificent party, but it ushered in both the New Year and the opening of the new DeSoto Hotel. Over a lavish banquet, guests talked about the new hotel, how it put Savannah on the tourism map and how it was a sign that the city was coming of age.

Guests feasted that night on oysters on the half shell, terrapin soup, roast pheasant, red snapper, and turkey. Set against a backdrop of Victorian splendor—chandeliers, plush carpets, and massive furniture—over 1,500 pieces of silver were used, along with fine china and pristine linens.

The hotel ushered in an era known as the Gay Nineties, an era noted for elaborate fashions, good times, and, for some, incredible personal wealth. Those who had the means traveled a type of circuit from one resort to another, and Savannah soon became part of that circuit.

The DeSoto also became the center of Savannah social life, at least for the wealthy, and many debutantes made their first introduction into a privileged lifestyle there. A common sight in those days was an elaborate horse-drawn carriage driven by a silk-hatted driver making the rounds between the hotel and the railroad station. Once at the hotel, the head porter, decked out in a derby, black polished boots, white gloves, and jacket, greeted guests.

Though pretentious by today's standards, rooms and private suites were equipped with electric bells, and those traveling without their servants could summon a maid, bellboy, or waiter to meet their every need.

ORIGINS

When Standard Oil tycoon Henry Flagler built the magnificent Ponce de Leon Hotel in St. Augustine, Florida, many Savannahians felt that Savannah needed a grand hotel of her own. Unlike any major project before, the hotel was built entirely with Savannah capital.

The new hotel was to be built on the corner of Bull and Liberty streets at the site of the Oglethorpe barracks. The barracks had been erected in the 1830s to support the Indian Wars in Florida.

Now the whole block from Madison Square on Bull Street to the north on Liberty and to the east on Drayton would be occupied. Elaborate materials were used in the construction: red and buff-colored bricks, stone, terra-cotta, tile, slate, marble, copper, and crystal. The floors were of rich oak and marble, crafted in fine detail.

Four million bricks were used in the structure, along with 300 tons of steel and 12,000 cubic feet of stone. By the time of its completion, the hotel spanned 40,000 square feet. The DeSoto boasted 300 rooms with tubs and showers, an outdoor pool, an eighteen-hole miniature golf course, an artesian well, and 8,900 feet of veranda stretching along the sides of the hotel.

Its Romanesque arches, verandas, tall, intricate chimneys, terra-cotta porches, and Tiffany glass windows became well known, and the hotel was heralded in popular magazines as the "most recognized architectural structure in the sunlit clime."

Yet, in spite of all the money spent and enthusiasm generated, the DeSoto was almost destroyed before she was completed. During Hogan's Fire of 1889, the building was endangered when flames approached and ignited the scaffolding. Only through quick thinking and great effort was the hotel saved.

The *Savannah Morning News* ran the following report January 1, 1890:

> The DeSoto is finally finished! It is a supreme monument, a modern hostelry that any [city] . . . of a dozen times the population of Savannah would be proud to possess, it is a Savannah enterprise, built with Savannah capital.

THE FAMOUS AND NOT SO FAMOUS

Not only did Savannahians and tourists frequent the DeSoto, but several luminaries visited the grand old hotel in its heyday. Among them were Katherine Hepburn, Babe Ruth, Herbert Hoover, Presidents McKinley, Taft, Wilson, and Harry Truman, actor Gregory Peck, boxing champ Jack Dempsey, Lady Astor, Will Rogers, and Gen. "Blackjack" Pershing.

In 1898, the year the Spanish-American War erupted, the hotel served as headquarters for the U.S. Army's Seventh Corps, commanded by Confederate war hero and nephew of Robert E. Lee Maj. Gen. Fitzhugh Lee.

Yet, as magnificent as it was, the hotel was rendered obsolete by two world wars, the Great Depression, and changing technology. Without adequate air conditioning and in need of renovations, she became too costly to run.

END OF AN ERA

On New Year's Eve 1965 the grand old hotel once again hosted a colorful ball. Partygoers dressed in World War I doughboy uniforms, raccoon coats, and Lindbergh jackets danced the night away with women dressed as flappers from the Roaring Twenties. By morning the party had ended, signifying the end of an era.

Journalist and columnist Ward Morehouse wrote:

> I sat on the veranda with the ease and authority of a paying guest, sat before its great roaring fire on chilly days, went frequently upon invitation to its elegant dining rooms, and visited in its luxurious suites during talks with the great and near great.

In 1967, the new DeSoto Hilton Hotel opened its doors, claiming to follow in the footsteps of the "sturdy, baroque Victorian DeSoto." The modern structure, towering fifteen stories, would have dwarfed the old DeSoto, and Savannahians were glad to have the new structure.

But years later many began to have doubts. Had a significant historic structure, now so dear to Savannah and part of the city's rich history, been foolishly leveled in the name of progress? Many think so.

James Moore Wayne, Savannah's First U.S. Supreme Court Justice

Two U.S. Supreme Court justices hail from Savannah. The first, James Moore Wayne, served from the Jacksonian era to just after the Civil War. The other, Clarence Thomas, was nominated in 1991 as the second black to serve on the bench and the second Savannahian. Both nominations created controversy, but both men rose above partisan politics to serve honorably.

Shortly after the election of Andrew Jackson to the presidency in 1829, a seat on the U.S. Supreme Court became vacant. Wanting to appoint a Southerner to the bench, particularly a Georgian, President Jackson nominated native Savannahian James Moore Wayne.

Wayne, 45, had served as a captain in the War of 1812, as Savannah's mayor (1817-1819), a Georgia legislator, a lawyer, a lower court judge, and a Georgia Supreme Court judge. In 1828, he was elected to Congress as a Jackson Democrat.

On January 6, 1835, Jackson submitted Wayne's nomination to the Senate and a few days later Wayne was confirmed. Swearing allegiance to the Constitution, Wayne took the oath of office administered by Chief Justice Marshall on the 13th. He was the first U.S. Supreme Court justice born under the Constitution. While his nomination met little resistance in Congress, it bred dissension—even resentment—in his native South.

In earlier years, Wayne would have been considered a Federalist. He favored a strong federal government and held the view, not yet solidified in the American consciousness at that time, that a citizen's chief allegiance belonged to his country, then to his region or state. Such sentiments were political anathema in most of the South.

REACTION TO THE NOMINATION

As soon as Jackson nominated Wayne, states' rights newspapers bemoaned the selection, taking stabs at his character. A Macon newspaper reported: "[A]ye, a seat besides Chief Justice Judge

Marshall!! Friends, imagine Judge Blackstone on the bench, and a ring tail monkey grinning at his side!!"

The *Charleston Mercury,* known for its sectional views, was not as coarse but stated that the nomination provided "very little satisfaction." And in an editorial, the *Columbus Inquirer* wrote:

> We live in an age of wonder. The man who was at best a second rate lawyer at the bar of Georgia; who was a third rate judge in his native state, is by some strange freak of fortune, or of folly, transmitted to a seat with the Rabbi of his profession.

Even Wayne's political allies greeted his appointment with little enthusiasm, possibly due to his recent nomination for governor of Georgia. In Savannah, the *Georgian* stated that "[we] would have preferred to have seen Judge Wayne accept that nomination, instead of the Federal Bench."

Leveling fewer charges than their Southern counterparts, Northerners varied in their opinions. The *Evening Mercantile Journal* in Boston wrote: "Judge Wayne has always been a distinguished politician and on that account, perhaps, the nomination is objectionable." But the *New York Journal of Commerce* stated that the appointment of Judge Wayne seems to be "accepted generally."

Displeasure with Wayne wasn't limited to the papers; several members of the Supreme Court harbored doubts about him. Justice Joseph Story stated that the court was now "gone." And Justice Smith Thompson of New York wrote that he feared for the fate of the Constitution.

If Wayne's nomination to the bench caused friction in the South, his refusal to side with Georgia when she seceded from the Union bred hate.

DRED SCOTT DECISION

Regarded as a Southern conservative, Wayne voted with the majority in the heated Dred Scott decision in 1857, which claimed that a black could not be a U.S. citizen and that Congress had no power to exclude slavery from any U.S. territory. Wayne didn't, however, totally believe in slavery, but felt that it should be phased out slowly. Chatham County court records show Wayne owned thirty-one slaves in 1821, but when he moved to Washington he employed Irish immigrants as house servants.

A few days after the Dred Scott decision, a New York newspaper described Wayne as an "intelligent, good looking Georgian" and a "radical on the slavery question who would dispute the right of any Northern man to have an opinion on slavery or its relations."

Often as a Supreme Court justice Wayne would preside in the circuit and district courts of the United States, often held at the Customs House in Savannah. The last prominent case he presided over in Savannah was the case of the slave ship *Wanderer* in 1859 and 1860.

When Georgia voted to secede in 1861, Wayne, a staunch Unionist, remained on the bench. He became so unpopular in the South that a Confederate court tried him in absentia and found him guilty, deeming him an alien of his native Georgia and depriving him of his property. His land was never confiscated, but turned over to his son, H.C. Wayne, a brigadier general in the Confederate army.

When Chief Justice Roger B. Taney died in 1864, Lincoln appointed Wayne as chief justice. He served until his death on July 5, 1867, at his Washington, D.C., residence.

Wayne was destined to become a somewhat obscure figure, particularly in Savannah, because of his unpopular views. Even the mention of his name in Georgia stirred anger for decades after the Civil War. Today, most Savannahians know of native son Clarence Thomas and his nomination to the high court, but relatively few know of Savannah's first Supreme Court justice—Judge James Moore Wayne.

Savannah's First Airmail Flight:
A Public Relations Ploy

For years Savannah prided herself as the city where the first air-mail delivery in the country took place. But decades later a Long Island, New York, pilot claimed the distinction. Not only was Savannah stripped of the honor, but the flight was deemed a public relations ploy.

Hoping to attract crowds and create headlines for the newspapers, Savannah Auto Club Association secretary and 1911 Vanderbilt Cup Race promoter George R. Herbert had an idea. In addition to the races that year, Savannah would be the site of the country's first airmail delivery. With the sanction of the U.S. Postal Office, the flight was officially designated "Air Mail Route Number 1."

THE FLIGHT

After barnstorming his way across the country, Beckwith Havers, a pilot from Austin, Texas, happened into Savannah at just the right time. With a pilot's spot to fill, Herbert hired the young barnstormer and arranged the specifics of the flight.

On a chilly Saturday afternoon on November 25, 1911, Havers stood next to his Curtis biplane at the old ball field on Bolton Street and was sworn into service by Savannah's assistant post-master. Nearby, 20 letters and 502 post cards were jammed into a satchel. Taking the sack in hand, the young Texan jumped into his plane. A convertible, with its engine running, waited for the delivery at the northwest corner of the park.

Climbing lazily, Havers' plane barely cleared the ball field's six-foot fence on takeoff. Once airborne, he circled over the field seven times, darting about to the delight of the growing crowd below. After a twelve-minute flight, he swooped down toward the waiting vehicle and dropped the mailbag within twenty feet of the car. The postman grabbed the bag, rushed to the post office, cancelled the cards and letters, and prepared for delivery. The post office netted a $2.84 profit for the entire delivery. The cancellation

An early-day Curtis biplane carried the first airmail from Savannah. (Photo courtesy National Air and Space Museum)

mark on the cards and letters read: "Aerial Substation, Nov. 11, 1911. Athletic Park, Savannah, Ga."

But Havers wasn't done for the day. After dropping the satchel, he buzzed the racetrack, located on what is now Victory Drive, pulling just a few feet above the lead car and racing it for a short distance before pulling away.

Looking for more mischief, Havers kept flying and finally spotted a company of sleeping soldiers camped in the far end of the park. Making a beeline for the camp, Havers flew in at tree-top level, zoomed down, and released a floor bomb. Several soldiers managed to grab their rifles and Havers sped away with the pop of blank rifle cartridges trailing behind.

Satisfied with making history and hamming it up for the crowds, Havers nested his plane gently on the grass in the middle of the park.

Not to be outdone, another pilot, Eugene Godet, climbed in his bamboo and canvas biplane and took to the skies, climbing to a then impressive and dangerous 6,500 feet. After fifteen minutes of flight, Godet began his descent, gaining speed as he approached. But he got caught in a crosswind, had trouble landing, and nearly crashed into a crowded parking lot. It was the last flight of the event.

LOCAL PRIDE

Decades later, a group of Savannah businessmen wanted to cash in on the historic flight. To confirm Havers' claims, the Savannah Area Chamber of Commerce contacted the U.S. Postal Service in Washington. But much to their dismay, an investigation revealed the unthinkable—Savannah had not been the site of the country's first airmail delivery.

Savannah had been "among" the first cities where airmail had been delivered, the Chamber was informed, but the honor belonged to Long Island, New York. Seven weeks before Havers' flight, a French-made monoplane piloted by Earle L. Ovington flew an experimental flight, carrying 640 letters and 1,200 post cards from an airstrip on Long Island to a clearing just 5½ miles away. As Ovington tossed the mailbag out at 500 feet, he secured his place in aviation history as America's first airmail pilot.

When word reached Havers he was livid. He denied the findings of the investigation, alleging that the New York pilot had not been officially sworn into service. Further inquiry disproved Havers' arguments and Savannah lost bragging rights to early aviation history. Both Havers' and Ovington's flights, however, were merely sideshows for what was to follow.

AIR MAIL COMES OF AGE

In 1918, the post office developed its own branch of airmail service, ushering in a new era in aviation. Equipped with vintage World War I aircraft, ranging from captured German Junkers to Curtis Jenny trainers to World War I bombers, the service finally decided to use the British-made de Haviland-4 to deliver its mail.

Initially navigating their aircraft by dead reckoning, the pilots of the airmail service established the nation's first air routes, developed radio-beam flying, were responsible for the installation of the first lighted runways and pioneered aviation weather reporting. But the breakthroughs came at a great cost. In 1921, 1,764 forced landings were recorded, about half because of mechanical failure and half due to weather. That year twelve pilots lost their lives. By 1927, the number had grown to thirty-two, nearly one out of every six pilots employed.

In 1927, the U.S. Postal Office dismantled its airmail service, giving the job to the newly established and more efficient commercial airlines, thus ending America's earliest, most colorful, and most romantic chapter in aviation history. Savannah, despite its one-time lofty claims, became just a footnote in the annals of aviation folklore.

Robert E. Lee's Savannah Days

Robert E. Lee graduated from the United States Military Academy in 1829 with the dubious honor of having received no demerits—an honor that stands unmatched to this day. Finishing second in his class and with an appointment to the elite engineer corps, he faced a bright future. Yet, any celebration was short lived. His mother, Anne Hill Carter Lee, died on July 10 at her Virginia home. And it was in Virginia that young Lieutenant Lee received his first marching orders. They read:

WASHINGTON D.C. August 11, 1829.

Brevet Second Lieutenant Robert E. Lee will, by the middle of November next, report to Major Babcock of the corps of Engineers for duty at Cockspur Island, in the Savannah river, Georgia.

Catching a packet in late October, Lee sailed for Savannah. He reached town on November 1, but the commander of the proposed fort (later named Fort Pulaski), Maj. Samuel Babcock, was away on an extended trip. With time on his hands, Lee was introduced to Savannah society by friend, native Savannahian, and former West Point classmate Jack Mackay. Not only did Mackay show Lee the ropes, but he welcomed him into the Mackay family home replete with three younger sisters. And Lee, only twenty-two, cut a dashing figure in his crisp, blue army uniform.

With the return of Babcock a short time later, Lee reported for duty. But Babcock suffered poor health and Lee acted as his assistant, taking over much of the responsibility. Essentially a mud and marsh island containing a few sand ridges, Cockspur Island challenged Lee's skills. Yet he was up to the task. Wading waist deep through muck and mire, and fighting mosquitoes, gnats, heat, and humidity, he oversaw the implementation of a drainage system and construction of the main wharf as well as developing a topographical sketch of the island.

Lee continued his work through the winter and into the spring of 1830. By May, he had constructed temporary offices and for the first time headquarters were established on Cockspur Island. In July Babcock left the island under the advice of physicians; he would never return.

After summering in Virginia, Lee returned to Cockspur Island in the fall of 1830. But during his absence a gale had destroyed much of his work. Lee, without Babcock and facing the decisions alone, started making repairs. But just as he was making progress, another hurricane raged up the eastern seaboard and blasted tiny Cockspur once again, setting the work back even further.

Finally, 1st Lt. Joseph K.F. Mansfield—Babcock's replacement—reported for duty. With the arrival of Mansfield, Lee again had the luxury of time on his hands. He began making more trips up river to the Mackay house and to the Isaac Minus house to visit the two Minus daughters.

Yet if any young belles had their eyes on the handsome young lieutenant, they were out of luck. Mary Custis, the granddaughter of Martha Washington and heiress of several estates, had already won Lee's heart the previous summer in Virginia. They would marry the next year.

In March 1831, with the survey of Cockspur Island completed, Lee received new orders to report to Virginia for the construction of Fort Monroe. Nearly thirty years would expire before Lee would return to Savannah for duty, and when he did the country would be torn by war.

LEE RETURNS

When the War Between the States erupted in 1861, Lee was on extended leave in Virginia. Originally not wanting to wield the sword, he was forced to choose sides. After refusing Lincoln's handsome offer of field command of the Union armies and resigning his officer's commission, Lee traveled to Savannah to assume command of Georgia, South Carolina, and eastern Florida coastal fortifications. In late 1861, he established headquarters at Coosawhatchie on the Charleston & Savannah Railroad.

While in Savannah, Lee was active building and supervising what sparse resources he had to meet the growing Federal threat to the area's coastline. He made repeated trips to Fort Pulaski, but found it woefully unprepared to meet an assault. Finally, on February 3, 1862, he transferred his headquarters from Coosawhatchie to Savannah to be closer to Pulaski.

Yet Lee's days in Savannah were brief. On March 3, 1862, Confederate President Jefferson Davis recalled him to Richmond.

So the soon-to-be-heralded Confederate chieftain left Savannah's defenses, only to have Pulaski breached and seized in four weeks. But in Virginia things would be different. For three long years he would lead the Army of Northern Virginia, and many brave men, North and South, would die before his mighty army was removed from the field.

POSTWAR SAVANNAH DAYS

In 1870, an ailing Robert E. Lee and his daughter Agnes left Virginia for a swing through several Southern states in hopes of reviving the general's deteriorating health. Arriving by train on the night of April 1, Lee met adoring crowds at the train depot.

Followed by throngs of well-wishers and bands playing military tunes, Lee traveled by buggy to Gen. Alexander Lawton's home on the corner of York and Lincoln streets. When the crowds persisted, Lee was forced to leave through the back door to get a good night's sleep. After staying the night at the Andrew Low house on Lafayette Square, he met with his old comrade in arms former Confederate Gen. Joseph E. Johnston and also managed to spend time with his old friends at the Mackay home.

On April 12, Lee and Agnes left Savannah by steamboat. They arrived at Cumberland Island, where Lee visited the grave of his father, Revolutionary War cavalry hero "Light Horse Harry" Lee, who died when Lee was eleven. On April 25, Lee stopped again in Savannah on his way back to Virginia.

Time was running out for Lee; he would live only six more months. On October 12, the South, indeed the nation, was struck when word spread of Lee's death. Suffering a heart condition since the war, he died at the age of sixty-three.

The *SS Savannah:*
Setting the Record Straight

In the early dawn hours of May 22, 1819, a sleek, new vessel steamed down the Savannah River. Her destination: England. Yet her destination wasn't the important part of the voyage.

According to the owners, the vessel—the *SS Savannah*—was on a historic journey as the first ship propelled by steam to cross the Atlantic.

She would be heralded as the ship of the future and receive high accolades, and generations of Savannah schoolchildren would learn of her exploits.

In 1818, a new schooner was under construction in a shipyard at Corlears Hook, New York. She was an impressive sight. Measuring 110 feet in length, she had a 25.8-foot beam, a depth of 14.2 feet, drew 13 feet of water, and displaced 320 tons. Her stern was square and her bow rose sharply upward to keep out of pitching seas. The ship's single funnel was fitted at the top with an elbow, which could be turned as necessary to direct the smoke and sparks away from the rigging.

CAPTAIN ROGERS

An eager seaman, Capt. Moses Rogers of Connecticut, saw the unfinished vessel and soon devised a plan. He would buy her, convert

The William Scarbrough House on Martin Luther King Jr. Boulevard in Savannah. Built in 1819 for William Scarbrough, one of the backers of the steamship *Savannah*, the house was sold a year later when Scarbrough's fortunes turned sour. Today, it is home to the Ships of the Sea Maritime Museum. (Photo by Karri Cormican)

her to a steamer, and sail across the Atlantic Ocean. If successful, the vessel would earn a place in maritime history as the first ship to make the transatlantic voyage under steam. But first he needed financial backing.

Support was hard to come by. Neither bankers nor businessmen were interested in what they called an experimental vessel. Finally, Rogers persuaded a group of Georgians to buy her.

"If you purchase the ship and outfit her for steam propulsion," he reasoned, "she will be the first ship to navigate the Atlantic under steam. The results for Savannah will be fame and an influx of capital."

The Savannah Steam Ship Company was formed to support the venture. With financial support secured, Rogers purchased the ship for $50,000. The only modification he made to the vessel was the installation of a one-cylinder, 90-horsepower steam engine.

In March, the ship left New York and was on her way to the Georgia coast, where she would be christened the *SS Savannah*. The *Savannah* was scheduled to steam toward England in late May.

ACROSS THE ATLANTIC

On May 22, the *Savannah* slipped out of the Savannah harbor and steamed for Liverpool. It was an uneventful voyage until she reached the Irish coast. On her approach, a British revenue cutter spotted the vessel with smoke trailing behind her and thought she was on fire. They gave chase for four to five hours in an effort to render aid before realizing their mistake.

In another incident, the *Savannah* confounded a British sloop of war that tried to force her crew to lower the American flag. Finally, after twenty-nine days and four hours the *Savannah* made port in England.

The ship became famous throughout Europe. There were even rumors of a trip to St. Helena to rescue Napoleon Bonaparte from exile.

From England the *Savannah* steamed to Stockholm, Sweden, and finally to St. Petersburg, Russia. In Russia, Captain Rogers tried to sell the ship to the Czar Alexander Pavlovich, an enthusiast of new inventions. But, to Rogers' disappointment, the Czar wasn't interested.

Rogers tried to find other buyers, but no one wanted to buy what was considered an experimental vessel. The ship returned home a commercial failure.

Back in the States, the *Savannah*'s engine was removed and she was put up for sale. For the next two years, she would serve as a transport ship between New York and Savannah, but her service would be short-lived. In just two years, the *Savannah* sank off the south shore of Long Island during a storm. She soon faded into the annals of maritime history.

In the 1950s, doubt emerged about the ship's claims. Many sought to refute the report that she had been the first ship to make the transatlantic voyage by steam. For proof, they turned to her log-books, now in the care of the Smithsonian Institution.

It appeared that the *Savannah* had misled history. Of the 700 hours it took to reach England, she was under steam for only 80 hours. The only time she steamed was when leaving and making port.

To many, this heightened suspicion. If she truly intended to be the first to make the transatlantic voyage, they reasoned, then she would have used steam for most of the voyage.

In fact, many concluded that she was merely a gimmick, intent on bringing the owners money. And it was only after the Czar failed to purchase the vessel that she was deemed a failure.

Supporters of the *Savannah* maintain that even though she steamed only part of the way across the Atlantic, she still deserves her place in history. They claim that the *Savannah* was under steam for twenty-five of the eighty-six hours it took to reach St. Petersburg, Russia, and that the longest time the vessel was under steam was for eighteen consecutive hours. They claim that she didn't use steam on her return voyage to the U.S. because of inclement weather.

But the *Savannah* has had the last word. The date of her departure for the transatlantic voyage, May 22, is celebrated as Maritime Day. Replicas of the ship have been built and placed in museums and, in spite of naysayers, she is still a maritime legend, locally, nationally, and internationally.

The Hurricane of 1881

On August 26, 1881, the *Savannah Morning News* ran a small article in the middle of page two. A storm was brewing in the Atlantic. Amazingly, no warnings were given. The same day, the U.S. Signal Corps reported a hurricane to the east, but no evidence can be found that a warning was issued. If it was, little heed was given. The results for Savannah were disastrous.

By mid-afternoon the next day, gale force winds were reported and sheets of rain began to pelt the city. By 9 P.M. it became apparent that Savannah was in the path of a major North Atlantic hurricane. And at 9:30 the Signal Corps reported sustained winds of 85 m.p.h., while barometric pressure dropped to 29.08 inches.

Before contact with Tybee Island was lost, its residents wired one last telegram. Winds were gaining strength and many that had tried to get off the island remained stranded. The steamer *H.B. Plant* tried to steam down river from Savannah in an effort to reach the island, but was turned back by winds and high seas. Tybee would not be heard from for over twenty-four hours.

In Savannah, shutters began ripping from their hinges and were sent hurtling down streets. Tree limbs snapped and tin roofs were lifted and whirled for blocks. Gas lamp globes were shattered by falling tree limbs, darkening an already black and ominous night.

By midnight winds blew from the east-northeast and horizontal rain met high tides. A storm surge swept into the streets.

At the northern end of City Market, roofs became little more than twisted metal as the winds continued to gain velocity. The Cotton Exchange building was slightly damaged but a large portion of its roof blew away.

On Drayton Street, several buildings had roofs ripped off; rafters were dropped in the middle of the street.

A house was swept into the Savannah River and its owners drowned. Close by, Addison Stokes' house began to fill with water. Fleeing to safety, he took his wife and two children to a neighbor's home. But that house too began to take a beating and was washed into the river. Addison's wife and the couple's two children drowned while Mr. Addison exhausted himself trying to rescue them.

As the storm surge and winds brought destruction, streets became blocked by mountains of debris: downed trees, telegraph poles, piles of tin roofing, lumber, bricks, and in time, bodies.

ON THE BAY

From East to West Broad streets, hardly a structure escaped the storm's wrath. The western end received the hurricane's full force and destruction was immense.

The outskirts of Savannah didn't escape unscathed either. There, too, buildings were destroyed and people drowned.

Morning finally came and by afternoon damage assessment began. Death and destruction were worse than feared. Not only did the storm take its vengeance out on people, but animals also suffered, and many drowned. Horse and mule carcasses floated through the streets.

Area rice plantations suffered as well. Both crops and life stock were lost. On several plantations, workers were drowned and buildings were tossed into the surging river.

A report from Thunderbolt came in: "Thunderbolt—scarcely recognizable by one who was there a few days ago."

Not only were bodies found in the city, but they also turned up in rivers and swamps, many of them swept out with the ebb tide. On Hutchinson Island nine bodies were found. On Rabbit Island a man and his wife, huddled in a new house, were blown into the river. They drifted down river for three miles before managing to get out.

TYBEE ISLAND

Finally, Tybee Island was heard from. The news was grim. Houses were completely destroyed and people were missing.

Many on the island had abandoned their homes and taken shelter on higher ground in the woods. Some fled to the Ocean House Hotel, but its lower floors flooded.

Ships didn't fare any better. Several ran aground trying to reach stranded residents. Boats, tugs, and ships in the Savannah River were tossed around like toys. Smokestacks were ripped from their foundations, masts were broken, some ships sank, and others were hurled into the marsh. One boat was lifted out of the river by the wind and carried to Randolph Street. A new yacht, the *Georgia,* was blown away and simply lost. A pilot boat, the *Belle,* was washed onto the marsh; it kept going and eventually wound up in the Wilmington River. Ships at sea had yet to be heard from.

AFTERMATH

Older citizens claimed that the storm's fury was unprecedented. It was compared to Savannah's storm of 1854, but was considered even more destructive.

According to the Signal Corps, the winds at the height of the storm reached 85 m.p.h. But this figure is likely too low given the destruction and loss of life. In addition, the Signal Corps anemometer and other meteorological instruments were blown away before the height of the storm, rendering an accurate reading impossible.

By the time the final toll was taken, over 700 coastal Georgia and South Carolina residents had perished. But Savannah would have little rest. In 1883, another hurricane hit, followed by still another in 1887. And in 1893, the Georgia coast was slammed by three major hurricanes in little more than a month.

FDR in Savannah

When Franklin Delano Roosevelt was inaugurated as president on March 4, 1933, he stepped into one of the worst catastrophes in U.S. history. Rampant unemployment, failed banks, bread lines, and families forced out of their homes became the norm. The country, paralyzed both economically and psychologically, struggled to survive.

Running against incumbent Republican President Herbert Hoover on a platform of a New Deal to bring the U.S. back to prosperity, Roosevelt won in a landslide, taking 42 of 48 states, immediately becoming the hope of the American people. And when he announced plans to visit Savannah on November 18, only nine months after his inauguration, the city was beside itself.

Roosevelt, particularly fond of Georgia, named it his adopted state, tracing part of his family lineage back to the state's colonial days. Years before he became president, he had purchased a home in Warm Springs, Georgia. It was later nicknamed the Little White House.

When news broke that Roosevelt would speak at Savannah's Municipal Stadium, City Hall received so many requests for tickets that the project was handed over to the Chamber of Commerce. Roosevelt was slated to be the keynote speaker at the closing ceremonies of the bicentennial celebration of Georgia's founding. The night before his scheduled arrival tens of thousands of Georgia and South Carolina residents flooded Savannah in hopes of seeing the new president. Yet, with limited stadium seating, many would be disappointed.

After a flurry of preparation, Savannah appeared to be ready. The day before Roosevelt's arrival, the city announced: "All persons with reserved seat tickets are to be in their place and seated at 9:30 or the right to a reserve seat will be lost."

Departing from Washington by train on Friday night, the president arrived the next morning at Savannah's Union Station. Before he even got off the train, he was met by an eager reception committee, including Savannah Mayor Thomas Gamble, Georgia Gov. Eugene Talmadge, and both of Georgia's U.S. senators.

As the presidential motorcade of a dozen cars, led by the president's open-air limousine, motored through the streets of Savannah, thousands of eager area residents lined the route. From nearly every building and home along the way flags snapped in the cool November breeze and solemn soldiers and marines stood guard. Waving his hat in appreciation, Roosevelt seemed to enjoy the lavish display of affection.

The motorcade traveled north to Broughton Street. From Broughton they preceded to Bull Street, where the bells of St. John's Church peeled out "America." From Bull Street they made their way to Gaston, then to Whitaker, then to Park Avenue. Traveling east on Park Avenue, the motorcade reached Bull again, then finally arrived on Victory Drive. Turning off Victory onto the stadium grounds, the parade entered the stadium through a private entrance.

AN ADORING CROWD

A capacity crowd, estimated at 40,000, already stirred to a fevered pitch by the U.S. 8th Infantry band, a 600-member choir, and two giant army bombers from Langley Field circling overhead, was ecstatic. A 21-gun salute announced Roosevelt's arrival.

Soldiers, firemen, and marines dashed about the stadium keeping the crowd in order. With every available seat taken, angry crowds threatened to storm the grounds, and police had to form a human barricade to keep them at bay. The craftier who were physically able shimmied up nearby trees to catch a glimpse of the president.

As Roosevelt climbed out of his limousine, he stepped onto red carpet, leading to the platform where he would speak. Nearby, a battery of reporters and photographers eagerly waited. On the grounds, close to the platform, 15,000 school children stood obediently at attention, waving tiny American flags.

But before the crowds could hear the president, they had to endure three other speeches from bicentennial committee members.

Finally, the president rose and slowly made his way to the

microphone. With this, thousands again stood and cheered wildly. As he spoke, millions nationwide listened on their radios.

Roosevelt delivered a historic speech. The day before, the United States had formally recognized the Soviet Union and had begun normalizing relations with the Russian government.

"I believe sincerely," Roosevelt said, "that the most impelling motive that has lain behind the conversations which were successfully concluded yesterday between Russia and the United States was the desire of both countries for peace and for the strengthening of the peaceful purpose of the civilized world."

As Roosevelt spoke, American and Soviet diplomats hustled around Washington, establishing diplomatic channels. And as Roosevelt hailed the Soviet recognition as an aid to world peace, its premier, Joseph Stalin, was systematically killing an estimated twenty million of his own countrymen in a political genocide.

Speaking out against critics of his plans to pull the American economy out of the depths of the Great Depression, Roosevelt said: "There are always doubting Thomases, those who fear change, those who played the part of the mule who had to be goaded to get him out of the stable."

He concluded his speech by praising Savannah on its rich history and contributions to the nation.

As the president left the platform, a reporter over heard him remark to Mayor Gamble and Governor Talmadge: "I told you I would come before Thanksgiving, didn't I?"

After leaving, Roosevelt traveled to Warm Springs for two weeks of rest, relaxation, and to study what he called "the problems facing the country."

Just hours after he left, Municipal Stadium was packed again as Mercer University clashed with the Clemson Tigers on the football field. Mercer won, 13-0.

Breaking the Color Barrier:
The Original Nine

"CITY TO SAY 'NO' ON NEGRO POLICE," read the head-line in the August 13, 1945, edition of the *Savannah Evening Press*. The message from City Hall was unmistakably clear. There would be no compromise, and no black police officers.

A letter from the Savannah Deanery of the National Council of Women, forwarded to Mayor Thomas Gamble a few days earlier, contained two propositions. The first was that the city "take under advisement the appointment of Negro policemen to the Savannah police department to serve in those localities that are exclusively Negro or nearly so." The second part of the resolution, calling for postwar planning to improve housing conditions among the black population, received a warmer response from City Hall.

It would take another two years before black officers would join the force. But when they did, they trained in secret.

After an exhaustive search for black candidates in February 1947, sixteen men were selected to undergo training twice a week for three months, and without pay. Finally, on May 1, 1947, nine of the sixteen were chosen. They were soon nicknamed the "Original Nine."

They were: James Nealy, John White, William Malone, Milton Hall, Leroy Wilson, Howard Davis, Alexander Grant, Jr., Stepney Houston, and Frank Millino. Of the nine, three were college graduates, two had attended college and all had earned their high school diplomas. Eight were World War II veterans.

JIM CROW DAYS

On May 10 the *Atlanta Constitution* ran a feature praising Savannah Mayor John Kennedy for hiring the first black police officers in the state. The paper claimed that the hiring was not a racial issue but one of common sense for the purpose of cleaning up gambling and vice in predominately black areas.

With satirical humor, it added: "Savannah is still in Georgia. We looked on the map to see. We also had our representatives make a further check. The buildings will stand, the river flows on to the sea, and Bull Street remains serene and beautiful. We expected nothing else."

While the papers lauded Savannah's decision, developments behind the headlines, however, were anything but complimentary.

The nine had to deal with an onslaught of bigotry. Taking residence in a barracks on West Waldburg Street, the black officers were forbidden to associate with their white counterparts. To complicate maters, they were prohibited from arresting whites or even patrolling their neighborhoods. Adding insult to injury, they weren't allowed to catch the bus wearing their uniforms. Once they arrived at their barracks, they would change.

Their beat, originally covered alone and on foot, comprised all of West Broad Street (now Martin Luther King Boulevard). Only in extreme emergencies, they were advised, could they enter areas east of their beat.

The Original Nine weren't just breaking the color barrier locally, but nationally as well. John N. Popham, a reporter for the *New York Times,* spent several days in Savannah researching a story. His dispatch was favorable, complimenting the work and character of the black officers. Yet, he did raise several questions about the political expediency of the appointments.

The black community, in Georgia and nationally, was gradually solidifying its political power after a 1944 U.S. Supreme Court ruling that recognized the rights of blacks to vote in primary election campaigns. Popham suggested that the appointment of the black officers was just as much politically motivated as it was intended to achieve racial equality.

BLIND HATRED

Not only did the Original Nine face open opposition, but blind hatred also reared its head. In mid-September, Ku Klux Klan stickers were found on several police motorcycles and squad cars, even at police headquarters on Habersham Street. The stickers, about an inch and a half square, bore the likeness of a hooded horseman next to the words: "Yesterday, Today and Forever." On the flowing robe of the Klansman were the letters KKK.

After the story of the incident broke in local papers, police chief J.W. Rogers issued an order prohibiting stickers, posters, or signs of any kind from being placed on police property. He also threatened to discharge any officer caught violating his order.

Small strides continued to be made when three more black officers were added to the force in December.

In time, much of Savannah accepted the change and hostility melted, with praise even coming from parts of the white community in the editorial and news sections of local and state papers. The Original Nine were credited with bringing the crime rate down in the areas they patrolled, and were noted for their professionalism and devotion to duty.

In September 1949, Sanford P. Butler took the reigns as the new police commissioner. The next month, he publicly praised the work of the black officers.

"I tell you what I found out amazed me," he said. "Those fellows, the 12 Negro policemen and three white sergeants, are doing a splendid job over there." He also lauded their work with the youth in their precinct, as "important missionary work," helping instill in them a healthy respect and appreciation for the police.

In the 1950s, black officers were allowed to move to the police barracks on Habersham Street and Oglethorpe Avenue. And more black officers were added to the force in the 1960s, but discrimination continued. Finally, in 1973, black officers on the force filed a class action suit against the city for discrimination practices, calling for equal pay and promotion policies. After winning the lawsuit, the Savannah Police Department became fully integrated and the last color barriers finally came down.

Today, the department employs 393 police officers, including 128 black male officers and 24 black female officers. In addition, there are 21 black sergeants on the force out of a total of 54 sergeants, 4 black lieutenants, 2 black captains, and 2 black majors. Each officer on the force, regardless of race or gender, is a credit to the fortitude, determination and courage of the Original Nine.

The Old Tybee Railroad

Long before carloads of vacationers and college students headed toward Tybee Island on Highway 80 for an afternoon of fun and relaxation, travel to the beach was arduous at best.

Early Savannahians choosing to make the trip would do so by sail. By the 1840s, many began traveling to the island by steamer. Though the steam packets provided greater access than sailboats, they were not without their drawbacks. They were slow, often missing their schedules, and only a limited number of passengers could make the trip.

Toward the end of the 19th century, Savannah's growing populace needed a quicker, more efficient way to reach Tybee, and native son D.G. Purse thought he had the answer.

In the spring of 1885, Purse acquired a considerable amount of land on the island with intentions of building a seaside resort. But he needed to bring in the masses to make the project financially feasible. And there was only one answer to the problem—a rail line connecting Tybee to the mainland.

In 1886, the Georgia General Assembly granted Purse a charter to build the line and the Savannah & Tybee Railroad Company was born. Purse hired a contractor and set April 1, 1887, as the line's completion date.

The building of a rail line spanning swamps, crossing marsh, and fording rivers, however, proved no mean feat. With short cuts made to keep ahead of schedule, workers laid track on shaky embankments along the way. Much of Purse's rail line washed away with the season's first flooding.

Hiring a new contractor, Purse made repairs and finally completed the project on November 3, 1887. It was only a partial victory. The vacation season had long passed. Purse would have to wait until the next summer to see if his experiment would work.

And work it did. By the summer of 1888, Savannahians began flocking to Tybee Island in record numbers, traveling the rails of the Savannah & Tybee Railroad.

Unfortunately, due to poor fiscal management and the heavy use of debt to raise funds, Purse ran into financial trouble. By May

1890, only three years after the completion of the line, the Savannah & Tybee Railroad filed for bankruptcy and was placed for bid at public auction.

The Central of Georgia Railroad made the highest bid, and the line officially became the Savannah & Atlantic Railroad. The popularity of the line continued. In fact, it flourished. During the early 1900s Tybee became the center of Savannah social life, and young and old alike fled the city in efforts to escape the stifling summer heat.

The Tybee Special pulled out of Randolph Street Station in Savannah and crossed 17.7 miles of track, arriving at the depot on Butler Avenue. When passengers unloaded, they headed for the beach, picnics, parties, or a day of exploration. By night couples danced cheek to cheek at the Tybrisa Pavilion, where more than a few young men knelt on one knee asking for a sweetheart's hand in marriage.

THE PLACE TO BE

Tybee also attracted the attention of the area's teenagers. For them, it was the place to be to pass away the summer months.

A newspaper account written a few years after the Pavilion closed describes a typical summer day at Tybee during that period:

> In 1914 the young ladies who enjoyed the surf went into the blue waters clad in home-made suits made of wool or heavy cotton. Puffed short sleeves were very well, but stockings must be worn, and large straw hats tied beneath the chin was the order of the day. The men wore stripped suits that stopped just above the knee and some of them had short sleeves in their bathing tops.

In its forty-six-year history, service was interrupted only once. On August 28, 1897, during the height of the vacation season, a hurricane pounded the island with little warning. With only one route of escape, hundreds were stranded. A lucky few made it out, but the rest were not so fortunate. In short order the track washed into the ocean.

Dozens, by many accounts, facing the wrath of the storm, perished. By day's end over 1,000 area residents were dead; many more were missing. Guerard Hewyard, a survivor, years later reflected upon that horrible time at Tybee, calling it a "night of terror."

By the next summer, however, the track was repaired and the line again was fully operational. It would serve another forty years without incident.

THE LAST WHISTLE

With the mass production of cars in the early 1920s and the building of the Tybee highway in 1923, it became only a matter of time before the Tybee Railroad became a relic of the past. By 1930, the line was losing money and in 1932 the train made its last public run.

Some missed the romance and excitement of the old locomotive, but many caught in the throes of progress gave it little thought. Finally, on July 31, 1933, the train chugged down the route one last time. On board were employees of the Central of Georgia Railroad headed to the beach for a picnic. It marked the end of an era.

An editorial in the October 1933 edition of the *Central of Georgia Magazine* lamented the demise of the old rail line. "Of course it had to go," it began.

> For years it hadn't been earning expenses, and lately earnings had been less than taxes to be paid on it. Hardly anyone was using it, but as we drove down that fine public highway we used to look at it and reminisce (occasionally). It had been a good and faithful servant, it had helped rear us as children, as slightly "older" children we had used it on "dance night" before the road was built, and we were really fond of the good old soul. But soon it will be gone, and we shall never see it again.

Lou Brissie
and the Savannah Indians

Two years after the end of World War II, the country was still piecing itself together. As it did so, U.S. Secretary of State George Marshall initiated the Marshall Plan, calling for billions in aid to help Europe's war-torn economy. Also in 1947, Americans were finally allowed to purchase the first new cars manufactured since the beginning of the war.

Air Force test pilot Chuck Yeager flew the first jet to break the sound barrier. And in Savannah, baseball was on everyone's minds as the Savannah Indians sought to clinch the South Atlantic (Sally) League pennant.

After a three-year hiatus due to the war, professional baseball resumed in Savannah in 1946. But 1947 would be the perennial season, a yardstick that all other seasons in Savannah would be measured against.

"1947 was the premier, honest to God, best season we ever had," said Tom Coffey, who covered the Indians for the *Savannah Evening Press.*

"The team took off and did everything right. They had Lou Brissie that year. He won over 20 games and had almost 300 strikeouts."

"That was a great year," said Delph Thorn, a longtime Savannah baseball fan. "The atmosphere in the ball park was good and the Indians had a lot of names driving it, like Lou Brissie. When he pitched he packed the park."

The Savannah ball club at that time was not affiliated with any major league organization but had a working agreement with Connie Mack's Philadelphia Athletics, according to Thorn. If Mack needed a player from Savannah, all he had to do was make the call.

BRISSIE'S LEGACY

Leland "Lou" Brissie was a baseball fan's dream. The 6-foot-4-inch South Carolina native could not only throw a blistering fast-ball, but was a decorated war hero as well.

One of only three survivors of his infantry squad that was wiped out by German artillery in Italy in 1944, Brissie was hit by shell fragments, shattering his left shin bone into thirty pieces and breaking his left ankle and right foot. Evacuated to a field hospital, Brissie somehow talked doctors out of amputating his left leg. But he was not out of the woods.

He spent the next two years enduring twenty-three operations to remove shell fragments and splintered bone, rehabilitation, and

Leland "Lou" Brissie as a member of the Philadelphia
Athletics. (Photo courtesy Philadelphia Athletics Historical
Society)

learning how to walk with a leg brace. His hard work and determination would pay off.

In August 1946, Brissie checked in with the Philadelphia A's, the
team he had signed with before the war. But he had to convince
Connie Mack that he could still pitch. Mack sent Brissie to
Savannah for the 1947 season and a local legend was in the making.

"He had a fastball that would be in the catcher's mitt before the batter had a chance to swing," recalls Delph Thorn.

Brissie could not only pitch, but also packed Grayson Stadium like it had never been packed before or since.

"Savannah had a tremendous turnout that year, nearly 200,000," Tom Coffey said. "On a Brissie night, you had to go out early to get a seat."

According to Coffey, the attendance for a game that Brissie started could easily fill the 8,000 seats at Grayson Stadium, with several thousand more spilling out on the grass between the grand-stand and leftfield bleachers.

Brissie went 23-5 in the regular season and set a Sally League record with 278 strikeouts. He also led the league with a 1.91 earned run average.

"That season was phenomenal," said Brissie, who now lives in North Augusta, South Carolina. "They gave me my schedule up front, at the start of the season, and told me that I would pitch every fourth day regardless. That was my real advantage. I knew how to prepare myself and I knew my schedule."

Brissie led the Indians to a second place showing, finishing just a half game behind Columbus. Though the team didn't finish in first, it was a force to be reckoned with in the playoffs.

CLINCHING THE PENNANT

The Sally League semi-finals began in the home park of the first and second place teams, with the second place team playing the third place team and the first place team taking on the fourth place team. The semi-finals were the best four games out of seven.

Savannah squared off against the Charleston Rebels and Augusta took on Columbus. Though Savannah won the first game against Charleston, the Rebels clawed their way back. They scored 3 runs in the 14th inning in game six and tied the series. The final game was scheduled to be played in Charleston.

In game seven, Brissie was called in and threw three innings of relief, saving the game and clinching the series. Savannah would now face the Augusta Tigers for the pennant.

Augusta, however, proved no match for the Indians. Savannah took game one, lost the second game and then shut Augusta down, winning three straight games, including a Brissie shutout. The Indians won the pennant and the loyalty of a generation of Savannahians.

Savannah continued to support the city's minor league clubs through the 1940s and into the 1950s. But with the emergence of television and other leisure activities, attendance fell rapidly. The legacy of the 1947 season, however, lived on.

"The '47 Indians with Lou Brissie were a great team," Coffey said, "but they left high expectations for Savannah fans. There was never another Brissie to come along."

Brissie, for his part, continued to pitch well. The day after Savannah won the Sally League pennant, Connie Mack called him up to the big leagues and on September 28, 1947, he stood on the pitcher's mound in Yankee Stadium facing the league-leading and soon to be world champion New York Yankees.

Brissie played seven years in the major leagues. His pitched his best year in 1949 with a 16-11 record for the A's and was named to the American League All-Star team. In 1951, Brissie was traded to Cleveland, where he finished his career two years later.

Few teams in baseball have had the impact on their fans that the Indians did in Savannah that year. Today, they live in the memories and minds of those who watched them and those who grew up hearing of their exploits.

Savannah's Customs House

On July 29, 1852, New York architect John J. Norris invited the public to review his newest, and, to date, greatest creation—the U.S. Customs House on Bay Street. As the thirty-one-star American flag flapped smartly in the summer breeze, federal, state, and local politicians and dignitaries applauded.

In less than ten years, the controversial trial involving the slave ship *Wanderer* would take place within its doors, bringing with it national press coverage and growing animosity between North and South; and when Georgia passed an ordinance of secession in

The United States Customs House, built in 1852, in Savannah. Gen. William Tecumseh Sherman stood on the roof and gazed over the city he had conquered so easily. (Photo by the author)

1861, the Stars and Stripes would come tumbling down, replaced by the Confederate colors.

In late 1864, Gen. William Tecumseh Sherman would stand on the house's rooftop and peer out over the city he had conquered without firing a shot.

In fact, few locations in the state are packed with as much history as this corner of Bull and Bay streets. Between 1736 and 1740, Gen. James Oglethorpe rented a single-story frame house on the location. On March 7, 1736, John Wesley preached his first sermon in North America in a small building on the back of the lot.

Savannah's first customs house rested at this site as well, but was later moved to a building on Commerce Row, next to the current City Hall building. From Commerce Row it was moved to Bryan Street between Bull and Drayton, then to the Cotton Exchange.

In 1837, the customs facility on Bryan Street, burned down. For the first time since its founding, Savannah was without a customs house. Shortly after the blaze, customs moved to the Cotton Exchange, where it remained until 1852.

On March 3, 1845, Congress purchased the lot on the corner of Bull and Bay to build a new customs house. Reluctantly, the city demolished the historic Oglethorpe structure still there, but most agreed time had rendered the house useless.

John S. Norris was employed as both designer and supervisor of construction, having been chosen over Charles Cluskey, a local favorite, who had already built the governor's mansion in Millidgeville. With the appointment of Norris, fears rose that he would exclude Savannah workers from the project. Yet, such fears were unfounded and Norris employed both Savannah workers and outside labor.

Norris is also known for his other Savannah structures: the Massie Heritage Center on the southeast corner of Abercorn and Gordon streets, the Greene Meldrim house on the northwest lot of Madison Square, the Mercer house at 429 Bull Street, and the Andrew Low house on Drayton Street.

AN ENGINEERING FEAT

The construction of the customs house was a mid-nineteenth-century engineering feat. Norris' plans called for the structure to be made of granite, iron, and stone. One story has it that the federal government, foreseeing the difficulties arising in the Southern states, had it designed as a fortress, but most historians discount the claim.

Built of Vermont granite (before Georgia learned of her own supply), the building is supported by six fluted, solid-gray columns 30 feet high and 3 feet in diameter. The columns were brought two at a time, lashed to the masts of schooners. From the river they were rolled 38 feet up the bluff to Bay Street. It took a month to inch each column up the bluff and another month to put each into place.

Norris designed the capitals of the columns with tobacco leaves, instead of the usual acanthus leaves, as a tribute to the region's distinct flavor. Made of a solid slab of granite, each column weighs approximately 15 to 20 tons.

Inside the customs house lies a magnificent winding staircase.

Tourists are often seen marveling at the staircase that has no perpendicular support except the wall to which it is attached. Each step locks into the next, giving the appearance of resting in midair. The house boasts 32-inch granite walls, iron rafters, and solid stone steps.

In a letter to W.L. Nodge, U.S. Secretary of the Treasurer, after the structure's completion, Norris wrote that the house was "completely fire proof inside and outside," and would last a thousand years. The structure's final cost totaled $179,000.

Originally, the building housed a post office on the first floor, the customs house offices on the second floor, and the U.S. Circuit and District Courts on the third, including offices for the judges, clerks, and district attorneys.

The customs house is an architectural marvel and a monument to its designer. It is the oldest federal building in the state and is on the National Register of Historic Places. Recognizing the historic importance of the site, the Georgia Society of Colonial Dames obtained permission to attach a plaque to the front wall of the building in 1935.

In 1964, a $179,000 contract for repairs and the installation of an air conditioning system was awarded.

In 2002, the customs house celebrated its 150th birthday. The building is a unique part of Savannah's history and the history of the nation.

Elvis Rocks Savannah

Blinking sleepily, nearly a thousand of the faithful passed around jugs of warm coffee and munched on cold doughnuts, wrapped themselves in blankets, and braved the night chill. By morning they all agreed it was worth the wait. The King of rock 'n' roll was coming and they would have tickets.

One day earlier, Monday, January 24, 1977, city manager A.A. "Don" Mendoza spoke to reporters. After two years of difficult negotiations, Elvis Presley was coming to Savannah for a one-night concert. He would perform February 17.

When the Civic Center box office opened at 9 A.M. the next morning, a line extended almost completely around the Savannah Civic Center, spilling onto nearby Montgomery Street. Up for grabs: 7,920 tickets and the chance to see a musical legend.

Just after noon, Savannah police locked box office doors and had the unenviable task of announcing that tickets were sold out. An estimated 1,000 people were turned away. But opportunity or greed, depending on your take, reared its head, and scalpers hawked $10, $12, and $15 tickets for as much as $100.

THE PRESLEY FAITHFUL

Presley arrived by private plane at Travis Field the night before the concert. Traveling by limousine to the DeSoto Hilton on Liberty Street, the aging idol was greeted by nearly a hundred adoring fans.

Yet the crowds were different from those that greeted him in his heyday. Instead of bobby-sox and pigtails, most wore designer jeans and had frosted hair with the first telltale signs of age etching their mostly thirtyish and forty-something faces. A generation that had come of age with the legend was still the Presley faithful.

Some in the crowd had witnessed Presley's first Savannah performance twenty-one years earlier, on June 25, 1956. Just after releasing his best-selling "Blue Suede Shoes, " "Hound Dog," and "Heartbreak Hotel," the Memphis native played Savannah at the old Savannah Sports Arena on Gwinnett Street just off Pennsylvania Avenue. Tickets sold for a whopping $1.50, $2, and $2.50. Playing two shows, Elvis brought in just over 3,500 fans for his first performance, and slightly less for his second show.

The twenty-one-year-old heartthrob, swiveling his hips and jumping about, kept the largely female audience on its feet. One thirteen-year-old girl fainted and had to be carried to St. Joseph's Hospital by police in what was described as a state of hysteria.

The local press, however, saw Elvis in a different light.

Covering the concert, the *Savannah Morning News* reporter wrote: "This is what we learned from the nerve-shattering experience. Women have discovered burlesque—and they love it.

"The men in the audience were strangely silent. They had sort of a subdued, even frightened look about them. They were sort of green around the gills."

On stage for only twenty minutes for each performance, Presley sang six songs, including "Blue Suede Shoes," "Heartbreak Hotel," "Long Tall Sally," and "I was the One."

When asked by reporters if rock 'n' roll was corrupting the morals of America's youth, Presley replied, "There's nothing to it. I can't believe music would cause anybody to do anything wrong. And what I do is nothing but music."

Two decades later, the King had come full circle: stardom, acclaim as a world-renowned figure, a drop in popularity in the late 1960s and early 1970s, then resurgence to the heights of the musical elite. But time was running for the aging rock 'n' roll singer. He would play Savannah just one more time.

LAST CURTAIN CALL

Two red spotlights pierced the dark and focused on the stage. Music from *2001: A Space Odyssey* began to play, and an overweight, middle-aged Elvis Presley took to the stage. A stream of roses from adoring fans followed.

Presley, in a white, rhinestone-speckled suit, not only bulged in the middle but was noticeably slower. But that didn't stop the singer or his fans.

Hamming it up for the crowds in his distinct style, he shimmied, jumped, and swiveled his hips. He worked his way through a dozen top melodies, bringing tears to the eyes of many. Engulfed in a glow of pink light, he climaxed the show with "My Way."

In response to an enthusiastic audience, Presley began throwing perspiration-soaked scarves and touching outstretched hands of those who managed to push through the dozen or more Savannah police hired to guard the stage.

Yet it was obvious that all was not well with the King. He failed to hit some of the high notes that had earned him millions and had to be carried along several times with the help of an eight-piece orchestra and a dozen backup vocalists.

After two hours, an exhausted Presley closed the concert with "Can't Help Falling in Love."

After his departure, the lights went up and a voice announced: "Ladies and Gentleman, Elvis has left the building." Not only was Elvis leaving the building, in just six months he would be dead.

"Elvis is Dead at 42," the Associated Press newswire read. The details were sketchy and at variance with some later reports. Presley was at his Graceland home in Memphis, it reported, and had apparently died of a heart attack. He was found lying on his bed, fully clothed, by his manager. After several attempts at resuscitation by emergency medical workers, it was confirmed. Presley was gone. Time of death: 2:30 P.M. on August 16, 1977.

While the Memphis coroner's office released its initial autopsy report that no other signs of disease and no signs of chemical abuse were found, Memphis detectives were denying reports of a possible drug overdose.

The debate would rage until the present. Did Presley die from natural causes or from complications of drug and alcohol abuse? No matter. For a generation of fans and millions of Americans, he was gone.

The news of Presley's death hit Savannah hard. Exactly six weeks after his death Elvis had been scheduled for a return performance at the Civil Center.

Savannah's First
St. Patrick's Day Parade

As the first wave of Irish immigrants landed in America during the early 19th century, hopes were high. Left behind were centuries of British oppression, poverty, and broken dreams.

But America would also prove cruel. Not only would these sons and daughters of Erin face hatred and discrimination in their adopted homeland, but economic opportunities would be scarce. With slaves laboring in the fields, many Irish immigrants, with few skills beyond farming, were unable to find work. Not able to compete against free labor, thousands of Irish workers had nowhere to turn except to each other.

A similar scenario played itself out in the Savannah area. In an effort to remedy the problem, thirteen Irish Protestants formed the Hibernian Society in Savannah on St. Patrick's Day in 1812.

Their purpose, stated in the Society's constitution, was clear and straightforward: "The maintenance of filial attachment for the Mother Country; the aid of distressed Irishmen and their descendants; relief of indigent widows and orphans of Irishmen and their descendants; the cultivation of good fellowship and the practice of charity."

To celebrate their organization's first anniversary, Hibernian Society members formed a small procession March 17, 1813, and marched to Independent Presbyterian Church to hear a message delivered by their vice president.

Five years later, the Society celebrated its sixth anniversary by holding another procession through the streets of Savannah. According to some sources, this may have been the first St. Patrick's Day parade in Savannah open to the public. A notice in the *Georgia Gazette* simply stated: " Parade today, 9 o'clock."

THE FIRST PARADE

Six years later—1824—however, is generally accepted as the first year that the parade was open to the public. Two days after the festivities, the paper ran an account of the parade in a single sentence: "ST. PATRICK'S DAY on Wednesday was celebrated by the Hibernian Society of this city with usual spirit."

By 1825, the parade's popularity had gained momentum, attracting both Irish and non-Irish alike. Adding to the excitement was a visit by Georgia Gov. George Troup, who agreed to take part in the celebration.

Around noon, the Society assembled behind its standard, accompanied by a band playing patriotic songs and Irish jigs, and marched to Governor Troup's quarters. With Troup joining the procession, they proceeded to the Savannah Theater on Bull Street.

Inside the theater, ladies filled the two lower tiers while the upper tier was jammed with men. Dressed in full military attire, members of the McIntosh Cavalry Troop, the Liberty Cavalry Troop, and the Georgia Hussars occupied the pit. Governor Troup sat in the center box, accompanied by a group of Revolutionary

War veterans. As the crowd chatted, a band struck up "Erin Go Braugh." An oration by Richard W. Habersham followed. After Habersham's speech, the Society members left in the same manner they had entered, escorting the governor back to his suite, then marching to the City Hotel, where they were dismissed until later that afternoon. The Cavalry paraded down several streets before finally breaking ranks on Bay Street.

Later in the afternoon, the Society, accompanied by Mayor W.C. Daniell, local and state politicians, and the town's clergy, reassembled for a banquet at the hotel. As music issued from Irish bagpipes, the group feasted, dined, and raised their glasses to patriotic toasts. Feasting lasted well into the early morning hours before the last reveler finally broke away.

With the exception of six years—1830, 1862, 1864, 1913, 1918, and 1921—the Savannah St. Patrick's Day parade has been celebrated annually since 1824.

No reason is known for the 1830 cancellation, but records do show that the Hibernian Society met on St. Patrick's Day morning that year, attended Mass, and later held a banquet.

In 1862, the parade was cancelled due to the outbreak of the Civil War. With area Irishmen, most loyal to the Southern cause, joining the Confederate ranks, many of those left behind in Savannah were too preoccupied with fears of a Yankee invasion to hold the parade. Likewise, in 1864 the parade was also cancelled because of war.

The next year, however, Savannahians experienced a different phenomenon, what some called an outrage. On March 17, 1865, only three months after Savannah fell into Union hands, the parade resumed. The *Savannah Republican,* published by occupation forces, covered the festivities, including an account of troops from the 9th Connecticut Volunteer Regiment, some even wearing green, marching down Bay Street.

After the Civil War, Savannah would hold a St. Patrick's Day parade every year until 1913. That year the celebration fell during Holy Week and was cancelled. But there was a procession of Irish faithful that made their way through the streets to Mass.

In 1918, the parade was again postponed. With the entry of

America into World War I in 1917, countless Savannah men were in uniform once again. When St. Patrick's Day 1918 rolled around, those remaining thought it dishonorable to hold the parade in the absence of those fighting.

And in 1921, the parade was cancelled to show solidarity with the Irish revolting against British rule.

Since 1921, the parade has continued uninterrupted, with attendance now reaching into the hundreds of thousands. From the handful of Irish faithful in 1813 to the modern-day throngs—many claiming to be Irish for a day—the time-honored tradition continues.

George Washington's Savannah Visit

❝**A** toast gentlemen . . . to the state of Georgia . . . to the new republic . . . to the president . . .❞

As throngs of Savannahians, regal and plain folk alike, lifted wine-filled goblets, blasts from Chatham Artillery fieldpieces rumbled across the horizon. These were just the first of hundreds of toasts made in Savannah on May 13, 1791, as Revolutionary War hero and America's first president Gen. George Washington visited Savannah.

Shortly after being elected to office in 1789, Washington wanted to get a better feel for public opinion. He made the monumental decision to visit every part of the country during his administration, and from October 15 to November 13, 1789, made a tour of the eastern states.

He postponed a trip to the southern states, but what described as a "spirit of jealousy" developed in the South. In May 1791 Washington began the southern leg of his tour.

WASHINGTON HEADS SOUTH

Washington's southern circuit took him from Philadelphia to his native Virginia. From Virginia he traveled through North Carolina,

Following George Washington's visit to Savannah, he sent two cannon that had been captured at Yorktown as thanks to the people of the city. The cannon are located on the north side of Bay Street in a small pavilion just east of City Hall. (Photo by Karri Cormican)

but didn't stop because North Carolina had not yet ratified the Constitution and was not yet a state. He stopped in Charleston on May 2 and later visited the tiny town of Beaufort.

On the morning of May 9, Washington and his entourage began the 80-mile carriage trip to Savannah. The trip was long and arduous. Washington's diary mentions vast rivers to be crossed by "rickety ferries" and expansive stretches of marsh, swamp, and mud. After nearly four days, Washington's party finally reached Purysburg (a small outpost near the South Carolina—Georgia border) near present-day Interstate 95. There, the president would spend the night and recuperate for the trip to Savannah.

The next morning, Washington was greeted by a Savannah delegation, five eminent patriots of the Revolution: the Hon. Noble Wymberly Jones, Col. Joseph Habersham, Savannah's first mayor John Houstoun, Gen. Lachlan McIntosh, and Joseph Clay. Accompanying them for the trip down the river were nine sea captains decked out in light blue jackets, black satin breeches, white silk stockings, and round hats with long black ribbons inscribed with the words "Long Live the President" in gold.

From Purysburg Washington rowed down the bug-infested Savannah River to Mulberry Grove Plantation to call on the widow of Gen. Nathanael Greene. According to some historians, Washington constantly fought off the area's gnats and mosquitoes, calling them deplorable. From Mulberry Grove, Washington made his way down the river by barge, finally reaching Savannah in the afternoon.

As the president approached the harbor, a flotilla bedecked in flowers was waiting to pay homage, and a band struck up "Here He Comes, The Hero Comes."

Colonel Gunn and General Jackson welcomed the president and then introduced him to Savannah's aldermen. Then an artillery company fired twenty-six volleys in Washington's honor. From the pier the president was escorted to his hotel by most of the city's male population.

IN SAVANNAH

After dinner, Washington traveled to Brown's Coffee House in the center of town where he greeted several guests.

The next evening a grand ball was held in his honor at the Filiature, a large meetinghouse on the corner of Abercorn and St. Julian streets. Soon, violins began to play and splendidly dressed gentleman and magnificently attired ladies waltzed. While some claim that the president didn't participate, others state that he cut a dashing figure on the dance floor. After he asked to be excused around midnight, the ball turned into a roaring party. Dancing continued until three in the morning.

The next day, General McIntosh and General Wayne conducted Washington on a sightseeing trip through the city. Admittedly, there wasn't much to see. The city's population at the time numbered around 2,500 and what houses there were rested mainly on the bluff. The squares were intact but were surrounded by empty lots. Savannah's boundary stood at Oglethorpe Avenue. To the south lay a dense forest of trees and brush.

Washington also toured the battleground of the 1779 Siege of Savannah with General McIntosh and spent time at the general's house. In fact, the only known structure remaining from

Washington's visit is McIntosh's house on Oglethorpe Avenue.

Fresh from his visit with McIntosh, Washington began making his rounds again. To list every ball, dance, and dinner held for the president, however, would be difficult. There were so many that Washington couldn't attend all of them.

The next day, a detachment of dragoons arrived in Savannah to escort Washington to Augusta. At Spring Hill, west of Savannah, the artillery and light infantry formed ranks for one final salute. Thirty-nine artillery volleys and thirteen infantry discharges echoed across the marsh.

From Augusta, Washington swung back through the Carolinas and into Virginia, completing his tour. During most of the trip military escorts attended him from towns along the way. In all of the major cities, he was welcomed by public addresses, the roar of cannon, the ringing of church bells, and other demonstrations of appreciation.

After returning to Mount Vernon, Washington was so pleased with his Savannah visit that he sent two six-pounder bronze fieldpieces. Upon one is inscribed: "Surrendered by the Capitulation of York Town, October 18, 1781." It was cast in 1756, during the reign of George II. Today, the cannon rests on Bay Street next to City Hall. Washington spent six more years as president. He died on December 14, 1799, at the age of sixty-seven.

Governor Talmadge Takes on FDR

"The poor dirt farmer ain't got but three friends on this earth: God Almighty, Sears Roebuck, and Gene Talmadge," Georgia Gov. Eugene Talmadge was found of saying. And from these very people, farmers and small-town Georgians, he harnessed immense political power.

With a slight build, horned-rimmed glasses, and a lock of dark hair that fell across his forehead, Talmadge epitomized the Southern politician. During political rallies he would discard his jacket, roll up his sleeves, and brandish a pair of bright red suspenders, claiming to be just an ordinary farmer, earning the nickname the "Wild Man from Sugar Creek."

Though he garnered support from rural Georgia, he didn't care if he offended the rest of the state. Shortly after his inauguration in 1932, he said, "God made grass for cows to eat, not for city people to chop off with a lawnmower."

"Slick feller from the city" became a favorite Talmadge idiom.

But there was one slick city fellow that Talmadge would take on who would prove to be his undoing.

On the heels of Talmadge's election to office, Franklin Delano Roosevelt entered the White House. With the country caught in the throes of the Great Depression, Roosevelt initiated what was called the New Deal, an aggressive program to reignite the nation's ailing economy.

Talmadge initially supported the president, at least publicly. Privately, however, he blasted Roosevelt's ideas, loathing both the man and his policies.

Talmadge, a firm believer in states' rights, resented the encroachment of the federal government. Speaking to reporters, Talmadge said he had already done enough to alleviate economic turmoil in Georgia. Nothing could have been further from the truth.

PRESSING THE ATTACK

After his reelection in 1934, Talmadge let everyone know where he stood. Not only did he openly attack the president's proposals but he assailed his character as well. In an *Atlanta Journal-Constitution* interview, he called Roosevelt a "radical in extreme form," and stated that it would be a national calamity if Roosevelt were ever reelected.

Referring to Roosevelt's crippling polio, Talmadge stated, "The next president who goes into the White House will be a man who knows what it is to work in the sun fourteen hours a day. That man will be able to walk a two-by-four plank, too."

Talmadge also voiced his opposition to the New Deal during a nationwide speaking tour. Traveling to Washington, D.C., he spoke to a national audience on CBS radio, calling Roosevelt's proposals "wasteful boondoggle, extravagant and the largest dole system ever known in the world."

In a *Washington Post* interview, Talmadge claimed that Roosevelt was destroying states' rights and was little more than a dictator. After leaving Washington, Talmadge pushed his agenda at political stumps in Chicago, Providence, Rhode Island, Sioux Falls, South Dakota, Bloomington, Illinois, Des Moines, Iowa, Philadelphia, New York, and Springfield, Illinois. Not only did Talmadge talk a good game, he backed his words with action.

When an old-age pension plan came up for a vote in Georgia, he vetoed it. When organized labor tried to consolidate their forces and unionize, Talmadge called out the National Guard to break their strike. He also hated borrowing, and thwarted any plan of the federal government to saddle Georgia with debt. When the federal government decided to lend funds to the University of Georgia for the construction of additional buildings, Talmadge blocked it.

"The United States has its eyes on Georgia," Talmadge said. "Georgia is conservative. Georgia knows you can't borrow yourself out of debt. Georgia knows you can't make water run up hill. Georgia knows you can't drink yourself sober."

POLITCAL SUICIDE

Yet, time was running out for the outspoken Georgian. Ineligible to run again for governor in 1936, Talmadge tossed his hat into the national political arena, attempting to unseat incumbent Sen. Richard B. "Dick" Russell. Russell, however, seized on Talmadge's lack of vision and was convinced that most Georgians supported Roosevelt.

"It's political suicide," the senator wrote, "to oppose the president and his policies."

Identifying himself with FDR and portraying Talmadge as a mean-spirited, scatter-brained hypocrite, Russell drew the political battle lines. Roosevelt, for his part, was elated to throw the influence of the presidency behind Russell.

When Roosevelt held a political rally in Atlanta, Russell attended. Talmadge, on the other hand, dodged the president and opted for a day of hunting and fishing near Savannah.

As the final months of the campaign approached, things heated up, with Russell seizing every opportunity to vilify Talmadge.

Talmadge seemed to confirm Russell's negative characterization, blundering in remarks to the press on several occasions.

Despite Talmadge's self-assurance that he could carry the state because of his support from rural voters, he lost. Russell won with 256,154 votes to Talmadge's 134,695. Ironically, Russell also carried a large percentage of rural Georgia voters. Roosevelt was delighted, calling Russell's win "splendid news."

Russell's and Roosevelt's political stars continued to shine. Russell served as one of Georgia's senators from 1933 to 1971. Roosevelt, elected president an unprecedented four times, led the country from 1933 to 1945.

Talmadge was finished, at least for the time being. Two years later he lost another bid for the U.S. Senate, this time to Walter F. George.

But in 1940, Talmadge rose from political defeat, returning to the governor's mansion for a third term, this time wisely refraining from attacking Roosevelt.

In a strange twist of political fate, Talmadge lost the governorship to Ellis. G. Arnall in 1942, only to win it again in 1946. But he died shortly before taking office. Few Georgia politicians have been as colorful or as controversial as the "Wild Man from Sugar Creek."

A Civil War Christmas: Shortages, Heartache, and Yankee Generosity

The year 1861 found America ripped apart by civil war. Though many Savannah boys had joined Confederate ranks and were in harm's way, Savannah had yet to taste war's fury.

When Christmas rolled around that year, Confederate hopes ran high. At nearby Fort Pulaski, garrison soldiers feasted like kings.

Pvt. John Hart of the Irish Jasper Greens, stationed at the fort for the first few months of the war, gives a glimpse of that Yuletide celebration.

"On Christmas night, everything passed off pleasantly amid songs and jokes from both officers and men," Hart scribbled in his diary.

The next night the two messes had an Egg Nog supper for themselves, we passed a pleasant evening, not leaving the tables until the drums warned us it was time to go out on roll call.

During the next week we were all in the best of spirits and passed a pleasant time all of us having received baskets of delicacies from the City. We lived that week more as Lords than Soldiers, we have enough to spare.

Savannahians, however, were not so jubilant by the next Christmas. Fort Pulaski had fallen and most Georgia troops were away on distant battlefields.

Sgt. W. H. Andrews of the 1st Georgia Regulars had already seen some of the war's worst carnage, including fighting at Manassas and the bloodbath at Antietam. He was in Virginia on Christmas Day 1862.

The troops spent the day in camp that Christmas, celebrating and playing practical jokes until Confederate officers put a stop to their festivities. Other soldiers weren't so lucky. Many describe horrible bouts of homesickness, cold, lack of food, and inadequate shelter.

SANTA RUNS THE BLOCKADE

Christmas 1863 hit Savannah hard. With the noose of the Federal blockade choking the South, supplies were low. Thoughts of Christmas gifts for kids seemed impossible.

One Southern mother, Sallie Brock Putnam, however, vowed to keep spirits up. She plotted the course Saint Nick needed to take to dodge the blockade and bring gifts to Southern children.

She wrote:

[G]ood old Santa Klaus has not lost his bravery, and that despite the long continued storm of war he will make his way through the fleet at Charleston or the blockading squadron at Wilmington, and from foreign countries, or perchance across the country from Baltimore, he'll pick his way, flank the numerous pickets on the lines and bring something to drop in new stockings.

By 1864, the tide of war had irrevocably shifted. Southern hopes were dashed after the fall of Atlanta. While in Virginia, Grant was playing a game of cat and mouse with Lee's beleaguered and outnumbered troops.

And in Savannah, the end of the war was a breath away. On December 22, 1864, after marching over 250 miles, the first of Sherman's blue-clad troopers entered the city.

Arriving later that day, General Sherman made his way to the Customs House on Bay Street. Taking to the roof, he gazed out over the city he had captured with relative ease. From the Customs House, the general rode to Pulaski House. While there, a nervous British cotton merchant, Charles Green, offered Sherman the use of his home for headquarters. It was also from the Pulaski House that Sherman penned his now famous letter to President Lincoln. He wrote:

Savannah, Ga. Dec. 22, 1864

To His Excellency, President Lincoln

Dear Sir,

I beg to present you as a Christmas gift the City of Savannah with 150 heavy guns and plenty of ammunition; and also about 25,000 bales of cotton.

W.T. Sherman Maj. Gen."

Sherman spent Christmas at the Green house on Madison Square, adjacent to St. John's Episcopal Church. Enjoying the splendor of the Southern mansion, he wrote a friend: "I am now in a magnificent mansion living like a gentleman but soon will be off to South Carolina."

On Christmas morning, Sherman attended services at St. John's Episcopal Church, creating a riff among the Confederate faithful. Savannahian Frances Thomas Howard described the events in his diary:

Christ Church was closed, but St. John's was open and filled to overflowing. The rector, Mr. McRae, was assisted by a Yankee chaplain and many of the communicants left without partaking of the sacrament. This has been a sorrowful Christmas day.

That night the general and his officers enjoyed a holiday banquet at Green's home.

But Savannahians had little to celebrate and little to eat. Many were destitute. The blockade had worked all too well, creating shortages of food, fuel, supplies, and medicines. Apples sold for

$50 a barrel, butter cost $1.50 a pound, and condensed milk cost $1 a can.

While Union troops enjoyed their first Southern Christmas, James L. Pierpont of Savannah, the composer of "Jingle Bells," lay in wait with the 5th Georgia Cavalry somewhere in the Carolina swamps, anticipating the Federal army's next move. For him, it would not be a merry Christmas.

W.H. Andrews of the 1st Georgia, whose unit had skirmished with Sherman's troops on their approach to Savannah and had recently evacuated the city, was bivouacked near the Savannah & Charleston Rail Road. Sick of war and tired of suffering, he wrote:

> Another dreary Christmas day in the army, making four I have spent in the army. Hope I never spend another one in the war, but from the looks of everything now, there is no prospect for war coming to an end.

YANKEE GENEROSITY

But not all was gloom in Savannah that Christmas. Yankee soldiers, it was discovered, did have a heart. On Christmas Day, a group of Michigan soldiers and their captain hitched mules to wagons full of food and supplies. Strapping tree branches to the animals' heads to resemble reindeer antlers, the soldiers distributed the goods to grateful civilians in the neighboring countryside.

This was the last Christmas of the war. In just four months Lee would surrender the Army of Northern Virginia to General Grant at Appomattox Court House in Virginia. Within weeks all Confederate troops would lay down their arms.

Finally, after four years of war, the country would be at peace for the next holiday season. But things really never returned to normal for thousands of families. At the Christmas dinner table, North and South, empty chairs sat for fathers, brothers, sons, and sweethearts who would never return.

— ⌘ —

Bethesda: A Lasting Legacy

George Whitefield arrived in Savannah in 1738 with one purpose: to provide relief for the growing number of the colony's young orphans. Earlier that year a yellow fever epidemic had wiped out much of the city, leaving dozens of motherless and fatherless children roaming the streets. Even before he left England, Whitefield had been persuaded by Gen. James Oglethorpe and John Wesley to establish an orphanage in Georgia.

But before he could begin, the Anglican Church recalled him to England for his ministerial ordination. While there, he persuaded the Trustees of Georgia to grant 500 acres of land on which to build the orphanage. He named it Bethesda, Hebrew for house of mercy.

Arriving in Georgia again on August 14, 1739, Whitefield immediately began searching for a spot to build his orphanage. He wrote: "It is my design to have each of the children taught to labor so as to be qualified to get their own living to be removed from the evil influences of the new colony."

Whitefield laid the first brick of the new orphan house on March 25, 1740. Appointing James Habersham, who came to Georgia with Whitefield from England, to oversee its construction, Whitefield began an evangelistic tour through the colonies. At the end of each service he would appeal for an offering to help support the orphanage, usually with good results.

Soon after Whitefield's departure, however, Bethesda suffered the first of a long line of catastrophes. Under cover of night, a Spanish raiding party stole a schooner laden with 10,000 bricks as well as supplies destined for the orphanage. Despite the setback, work and construction continued.

Whitefield traveled the length and breadth of the colonies. He met Benjamin Franklin in Philadelphia. Franklin showed considerable interest in the orphanage and wanted to move it to Philadelphia, where it could benefit from the city's rich supply of materials and resources. When Whitefield refused, Franklin became indignant, claiming that he would no longer offer his support. But he would soon have a change of heart.

"I happened soon after to attend one of his [Whitefield's] sermons," Franklin wrote,

> in the course of which I perceived that he intended to finish with a collection and I silently resolved that he get nothing from me. I had in my pocket a handful of copper money, three or four silver dollars and five pistols of gold. As he proceeded I began to soften and I concluded to give the coppers. Another stroke of his oratory made me ashamed of that and determined me to give the silver; and he finished so admirably that I emptied my pocket into the collector's dish, gold and all.

In a dual mission of evangelism and raising funds for Bethesda, Whitefield preached in every colony in British North America and nearly every town and hamlet in Wales and Scotland, crossing the Atlantic thirteen times. Upon Whitefield's death in 1770, it was estimated that he had publicly preached 18,000 times during his thirty-four-year ministerial career. After Whitefield's death, Bethesda's future seemed uncertain. But he had already made provision to keep his dream alive.

THE DREAM LIVES ON

In his will, Whitefield left the orphanage and nearly his entire estate to his English friend Lady Hastings, the Countess of Huntingdon, who pledged to continue Whitefield's work. But tragedy would soon strike.

Fire destroyed Bethesda's main building and damaged others. Delving into her private fortune, Lady Huntingdon began an ambitious rebuilding program. She died in 1791 just after its completion.

No provision had been made for Bethesda after Huntingdon's death and ownership of Bethesda transferred to the state. Ten years passed before the orphanage became fully operational again.

In 1805, the Union Society, a benevolent organization for widows and orphans, took charge of Bethesda, ushering in a new era. Yet, misfortune struck again.

The same year a hurricane slammed the tiny orphanage, leveling its new buildings. Soon after, a portion of the land was sold and the boys moved to quarters in the city. In 1817, they were housed at the Chatham Academy, where they received a presidential visit from James Monroe during his 1819 Savannah tour.

In 1831, the boys moved to Springfield, but returned in 1837 to

Savannah, where they boarded with John Haupt at the Savannah Academy and were instructed by the Rev. George White.

By the 1850s, the Union Society began to flourish, growing to 553 members. Bethesda's fortunes also improved as its eleven boys returned to the original site, new buildings, and sixty acres of cultivated land. With the Union Society growing to 748 members in 1860, and with forty-one boys living at Bethesda, the future looked bright. But their stay would be brief. War would erupt, and the officers and members of the Union Society would join Confederate ranks in droves, heading to the front. Future building projects were abandoned and the boys were left without a teacher. In 1862, the 7th Georgia Battalion established its headquarters at the site and set up a hospital in one of the smaller buildings.

With the influx of troops to Bethesda, the boys were moved to Jefferson County, 107 miles from Savannah, where they would stay for the balance of the war.

SPARED THE TORCH

When Federal soldiers came upon Bethesda in late 1864, they were preparing to put it to the torch. But they spared the facility when they learned that the orphanage was under the care of the Union Society.

Throughout the war Bethesda remained intact, except for the loss of a few horses and livestock. In 1867, the Union Society regained control of the land, and it has been used as an orphan home ever since.

Though catastrophes, fires, and hurricanes have destroyed all of the original buildings, a replica of the Whitefield chapel was built in 1924. It still stands.

Today, Bethesda is a private, non-profit organization that is funded through private organizations, foundation grants, and endowments. The orphanage also receives per diem reimbursements from the Department of Human Resources for boys in state custody.

Bethesda has the distinction of being the oldest operational orphanage in the country. Nearly 10,000 boys have passed through her doors. Bethesda continues to thrive, keeping George Whitefield's dream alive.

Dishonesty in High Places: The Yazoo Land Fraud

With a hangman's noose in hand and scores of people rallying behind, Miles Jennings led a bloodthirsty mob past the Oglethorpe County Courthouse. Their intended victim: Oglethorpe County state representative Musgrove.

Having been tipped off at the last minute, Musgrove barely escaped with his life. Yet, this scene repeated itself in virtually every county in Georgia, including Chatham. Throughout the state in 1795 angry mobs sought those elected officials who had betrayed them in the biggest swindle ever against the people of Georgia, possibly the country. It would soon be called the Yazoo Land Fraud, named after a small stream that feeds into the Mississippi River.

Originally, Georgia's boundaries stretched from the Savannah River all the way to the Mississippi, covering millions of acres. Shortly after the end of hostilities with Great Britain in 1789, various efforts were made to try to purchase these western lands. Some of these efforts were legitimate, but many were not. All had one thing in common: the support of men in high places.

One group trying to acquire the land was the Virginia Yazoo Land Company, whose president was Patrick Henry. Henry's company was the first to make application to the Georgia General Assembly for the purchase of the lands. Though he was honest, those under him were not.

Another company, the South Carolina Yazoo Company, led by the most unscrupulous men who ever dabbled in American business and politics, also made application to buy the lands. After intense lobbying, the land-grabbers successfully persuaded enough legislators to pass the Yazoo land bill. But the bill never made it past the governor's desk.

A second, similar bill was presented before the legislature by four different companies—the Georgia Company, the Georgia Mississippi Company, the Upper Mississippi Company, and the Tennessee Company—asking for grants to purchase 35 million acres. Again the bill passed in the legislature, but Gov. George Mathews vetoed it.

Yet the land-grabbers did anything but bow out gracefully. They continued to harness funds and political power, using blackmail and coercion to win support. They bribed members of the legislature with funds as well as land. Those who refused to violate their consciences and support the sale were paid to go home and remain away from the legislature.

Judges were also persuaded to join their ranks, as were members of Congress. Included in the conspiracy was a U.S. Supreme Court justice, reported to have received $25,000 for his support, a U.S. District Court judge, several prominent military leaders, and James Gunn, one of Georgia's U.S. senators, who was seen bullying Georgia legislators with a loaded bull whip.

Unsurprisingly, the Yazoo land bill passed in the House for the third time. Bowing to enormous pressure and even threats, Governor Mathews, with two sons standing to profit handsomely from the sale, reluctantly signed the bill, making it law. Thirty five million acres were split between the four companies for $500,000, or only one and a half cents per acre. It stirred the uproar of the century.

GEORGIANS DEMAND ACTION

Outraged, the people of Georgia demanded action, and when the politicians were slow to respond, they took matters into their own hands. They issued threats to many of the legislators who had capitulated to the greedy companies. There was even a price placed on the governor's head. While the governor survived physically, he died politically. Soon, he would be out of office.

The masses held what many called indignation meetings in public squares, dispatching bands of citizens to find those who had voted in favor of the sale. Many legislators fled to South Carolina for refuge, barely escaping death. But one legislator wasn't so lucky. He was found shot to death in an obscure cabin in the Carolina woods.

At the people's prodding, grand juries were swift to assemble, and towns and counties passed resolutions denouncing the land sale. With public mistrust of elected officials soaring, the people turned to General Twiggs, senior military officer in the state, for help. When Twiggs waffled, they turned to senator and Revolutionary War hero Gen. James Jackson, who had already denounced the sale in the U.S. Senate.

With Jackson championing their cause, the tide finally appeared to be changing. Not to be outdone, the land-grabbers offered Jackson a half million acres for his support. When he refused, they turned to harassment and death threats. But Jackson was fearless. Before the full U.S. Senate he denounced the schemes as "a speculation of the darkest character" and an act of "deliberate villainy."

Spearheading the people's agenda, Jackson resigned his Senate seat to run for the state legislature, where he would chair a committee that would try to nullify the Yazoo land sale. With a new governor in office and a newly elected anti-Yazoo legislature, the committee declared the bill a fraud and recommended that it be repealed. The legislature concurred, stating "the fraud practiced to obtain it [land] made it a nullity itself, and not binding or obligatory upon the people of this state."

On February 13, 1796, newly elected governor Jared Irwin signed the Rescinding Act, finally nullifying the sale.

THE FIRE OF HEAVEN

On February 15, the legislature ordered that a large fire be kindled in front of the statehouse and that it be lit from the sun by a burning glass in order to incinerate the obnoxious papers with the fire of heaven. With the fire gaining intensity, a clerk proclaimed, "God save the State! And may every attempt to injure them perish as these corrupts acts now do!"

After further denunciation of the corruption, the Yazoo papers were thrown into the fire and burned to ashes.

The four companies tried to defeat the Rescinding Act, but it was in vain. The issue lingered for a few more years before finally being put to rest. A hero of the people, General Jackson was elected Georgia's governor on January 12, 1798.

The Atlantic Lifeline:
Building Liberty Ships

November 20, 1942: U.S. troops inflict heavy damage on Japanese positions in the Solomon Islands, British army units close in on Hitler's premier military tactician in North Africa, Field Marshal Erwin Rommel, and in Savannah the *SS Oglethorpe* is christened.

That day, after listening to speeches by Sen. Walter F. George and Adm. Howard L. Vickery, thousands watched a bottle of 1857 Brut-Curee champagne smash across the bow of the 10,500-ton ribbon-laden *Oglethorpe.*

As the vessel slid down the ways into the chilly Savannah River, she became the first Liberty ship to be completed and launched in Savannah during World War II.

In what has been described as the largest shipbuilding enterprise in American history, 2,751 Liberty ships were built at fourteen shipyards across the country in just three and half years. And Savannah contributed mightily. By war's end, nearly 100 Liberties would be built there, slip into the Savannah River, and circle the globe, carrying much-needed war supplies to Allied troops locked in a death struggle with the armies of the Axis powers.

FDR DECIDES TO BUILD SHIPS

Just before the Japanese attack on Pearl Harbor in 1941, President Franklin D. Roosevelt ordered the U.S. Maritime Commission to begin a massive emergency shipbuilding program. Across the nation, the Commission, flush with funds, began to award lucrative shipbuilding contracts.

Savannah would also get a piece of the pie. Savannah Shipyards, Inc. was awarded a half-dozen shipbuilding contracts, but the contracts required special provisions for both management and the capital structure of the company.

On both counts, the company fell short. To remedy the problem, new management was brought in, the company was restructured and renamed Southeastern Shipbuilding Corporation. And what an undertaking it was.

The *Lyman Hall* is launched on February 6, 1943. The ship was named for one of Georgia's signers of the Declaration of Independence. (Photo courtesy Georgia Historical Society)

Southeastern Shipbuilding pumped millions of dollars into Savannah's Depression economy, providing thousands of jobs and changing Savannah demographics forever. New housing was constructed, and workers moved into places like Pine Gardens, Tattnall Homes, and Deptford Place. By the end of the war over 45,000 workers had passed through the doors of Southeastern Shipbuilding Corporation.

Workers flocked to Savannah in droves from Springfield, Blitchton, Pembroke, Clyo, Statesboro, Brooklet, and a dozen other South Georgia towns to work at the shipyard. Not only came men, but women as well, many experiencing the outside work world for the first time.

Most of the workers had little idea how to build ships. Many had never even seen a ship before. In the plant, workers would cry out "round windows," instead of portholes, the "pointed end" instead of bow, and "right, left," instead of starboard and port. It was comical, but also dangerous. One former worker told of sheet metal flying across the plant and men operating machinery with little or no instruction.

They learned, however, and in time cranked out an impressive succession of ocean-going vessels. But the ships were not without their problems, either. Given the Liberty ships' high rate of attrition, they were designed for no more than five years of service. In addition, the speed of construction and the new technology of arc welding caused structural failures in many vessels.

PROBLEMS AT SEA

Once underway, some Liberty ships actually broke in half; others had their propellers fall off in mid-ocean.

In the rough, frigid North Atlantic, Liberties became particularly vulnerable to stress fractures. A crack would start in a ship's hull and race across the ship through welded joints. In time, tougher steel was employed and rivets reinforced vital welded areas, eliminating most of the structural problems.

The average Liberty ship measured 441 feet, 6 inches in length, had a beam of just under 57 feet, and displaced just over 14,000 tons. They had a 28-foot draft, and at top speeds steamed only 11 knots. Most Liberties were equipped with light armament, a 20mm and 40mm gun, as well as a 3-inch, 50-caliber gun and 5-inch, 38-caliber cannon. A Liberty ship's five holds could carry over 9,000 tons of cargo, plus airplanes, tanks, and locomotives lashed to its deck. She could carry 2,840 jeeps and 440 tanks.

HONORING PAST HEROES

The names of Liberty ships built in Savannah read like a Georgia history book. Joining the *Oglethorpe* on the high seas were the *James Jackson, George Walton, Lyman Hall, Button Gwinnett, John Milledge, Florence Martus, Robert Toombs, Casimir Pulaski, Joseph Brown, George Whitefield, Joseph Habersham, Juliette Gordon Low,* and *Francis S. Bartow,* among others.

Though similar in design and dimensions, each Southeastern ship met a different fate. The *Oglethorpe*, the pride of the shipyard,

crossed paths with a German U-boat in the Atlantic, was torpedoed, and sank. Eleven Savannahians on board perished.

The *George Walton* caught fire 350 miles off the Oregon coast,
was abandoned, and later taken in tow, but the towline broke and
she sank 40 miles from shore. The *Jonas Lie* and the *John A.
Treulton* were also torpedoed by U-boats. The *Jonas Lie* went down,
but the captain of the *John A. Treulton* beached his vessel near
South Hampton on the English Channel, where she was refloated.

Other Liberty ships owed their demise to Mother Nature. A
typhoon drove the *William W. Seaton* for several days before she
finally ran aground off Kaohsiung, Taiwan, and was abandoned.
Ninety miles east of Midway Island, the *James Swan* ran aground
and broke in two.

Yet, others survived, serving in some of the fiercest campaigns
of the war, including D-Day and fighting in the Pacific.

As World War II came to a grueling end, so did the construction
of Liberty ships. In the fourteen shipyards scattered across the
nation's coasts that built Liberties, workers were laid off and plants
quickly dismantled. And in Savannah, on September 14, 1945,
Southeastern Shipbuilding christened its last vessel.

LAST CHRISTENING

Around noon, thousands of Savannahians and shipyard employees gathered to watch the christening of the *SS Half Knot.* The Rev.
Middleton S. Barnwell, bishop of the Episcopal Diocese of
Georgia, who pronounced the benediction of the yard's first vessel
three and a half years earlier, began the ceremony. Praising the dedication and fortitude of the shipyard workers, he prayed that new
doors of service would open so that they could continue to be useful and play a part in building a greater America and a New World.

Applauding in the crowd that day were several prominent
Savannahians: Hershal V. Jenkins, president of the *Savannah
Morning News* and *Savannah Evening Press;* William Murphy,
chairman of the board of C&S Bank; Savannah Electric and Power
president C.C. Curtis; U.S. district attorney J. Saxton Daniel, and
numerous state and local politicians.

As the ceremony continued, solemn workers, with blowtorches

in hand, sliced through metal, reducing partly completed ships to scrap. Equaling nearly three completed vessels, 150,000 tons of scrap metal was loaded on boxcars and hauled away.

An account in a local paper described the somber occasion:

> In the main, it was the usual type of launching ceremony so familiar to Savannahians. Gay bunting floated in the breeze, the band played martial airs and there was the customary breaking of a good bottle of champagne across the bow. But there was a difference—it was the final launching, the end of a job well done. You could see the tinge of sadness in the faces of the workmen who flocked around.

Just after three in the afternoon, the 338-foot AV-1 *Half Knot* slid down the ways, splashing into the Savannah River. Tugs escorted her to the wet dock for final completion. There were to be trial runs before she was handed over to the Maritime Commission. The *Half Knot*'s launching marked the end of an era.

In its wartime history, Southeastern built eighty-eight Liberty ships and eighteen AV-1 vessels. The company generated $112 million in payroll. A total of 46,766 workers passed through Southeastern's doors in three and a half years. The highest employment came in December 1943 when the shipyard boasted 15,303 workers, not including subcontractors. Of the $112 million earned, workers bought $11 million worth of War Bonds from Uncle Sam.

A SHIP'S REBIRTH

After the war large numbers of Liberties were scrapped, while others were added to the nation's Defense Reserve fleet. Some were sold to foreign nations, namely, England, Italy, Greece, France, Norway, and China.

But one Savannah-built Liberty would be born again. After limping to Erie, Pennsylvania, the rust-laden *SS Harry S. Glucksman* was stripped to her bare hull. Later towed to Ohio, the ship was re-fabricated. She was filled with plastic foam and fitted with eight outboard motors. The motors allowed her to maneuver sideways and up and down waterways, clearing minefields as wide as her own length. On the bow, a bridge mounted on shock absorbers was constructed.

Converted to a minesweeper and re-designated *FY 66* (USN) in August 1969, the vessel plied the jungle rivers of Vietnam clearing mines, serving until the end of hostilities.

SOUTHEASTERN DISMANTLED

On October 13, 1947, the U.S. government sold Southeastern's property, approximately ninety acres, to the Savannah Port Authority and Industrial Committee for $357,112. The six ways that had launched so many ships quickly rotted and were dismantled.

Two-thirds of all the cargo that left the United States during the Second World War did so on Liberty ships. Two hundred Liberties were sunk by enemy action, but so many filled the seas that German U-boats exhausted themselves trying to keep track of them all. The sea lanes remained open and the Liberties help usher in an Allied victory.

Ted Turner:
To the America's Cup and Beyond

Who knows what kid you may be able to inspire or influence when working with young people? Maybe a future police officer, or fire fighter, maybe a teacher or physician, or maybe a future America's Cup champion and world-renowned business tycoon.

Savannahian John McIntosh, age seventy-seven, who has been teaching kids how to sail for a half century, never imagined how one precocious boy under his helm would reach such heights.

McIntosh first met Edward Robert Turner III, nicknamed "Teddy," in 1950 when Turner was only twelve years old. Ted's father, Ed Turner, had moved his family from Cincinnati to Savannah three years earlier to expand Turner Outdoor Advertising, the family business.

About the same time, the Savannah Yacht Club had recently reformed after shutting down during World War II, and developed a program to teach area kids how to sail.

"We convinced parents of ten boys to buy Penguins—little 11-12 foot dinghies," McIntosh said. "Teddy and a group of boys, David Scales, Lee Thompson, Carl Helfrich, and others, enrolled."

The boys were taught the basics of sailing and then how to race. In time, according to McIntosh, all ten became good sailors, but Ted developed into a fierce competitor.

As Ted was learning to sail and passing through his teenage years, his father was busy building his business. Though he had been a sailor and had owned a schooner, Ed Turner did not sail competitively. As a result, Ted spent a great deal of time with the McIntosh family and traveled with them to several sailing regattas.

"Teddy's father was a good friend of mine," said McIntosh. "I developed a real interest in Teddy and he became an excellent sailor. When he was fourteen, he crewed with me in the South Atlantic Yacht Race."

According to McIntosh, Ted's sailing interest continued to build and he kept pestering his dad to buy him a new boat. Eventually conceding, he bought Ted an older 19-foot lighting class sailboat. Turner would put it to good use.

"From there," recalls McIntosh, "Teddy got better and better."

At this point, Turner began to show the qualities that would enable him to win the America's Cup race as well as build a billion-dollar empire.

"He was an extremely competitive, aggressive, and brash young man," McIntosh said. "When you watched him sail as a teenager, you could see his tenacity. He was a fast learner, learned the rules, the techniques, and how to get the maximum out of his boat. He had a fierceness and competitiveness seldom seen in boys that age."

Though Ted sailed Savannah waters in the summer, during the academic year he attended McCallie Military Academy in Chattanooga from the seventh grade until his graduation in 1956, earning the nickname "Terrible Ted" for his pranks, antics, and behavior.

After graduating from McCallie, Turner began his freshman year at Brown University and continued to sail, joining the Brown Yacht Club. But the young man who would one day become the founder of Cable News Network and Turner Network Television and donate $1 billion to the United Nations was also known for his other extracurricula collegiate activities.

Halfway through his junior year, the college asked him to leave after he was caught with a co-ed in his private quarters.

During his college years, however, Turner's sailing prowess came full circle. When he was a freshman at Brown, he crewed with McIntosh and McIntosh's wife, Barbara, in the Lighting North American Championship in Connecticut and at the President's Cup in New Zealand.

While in Norton, Connecticut, Turner's next-door neighbor was Bob Bavier, editor of *Yachting Magazine*. According to McIntosh, Bob got to know Turner very well and introduced him to the national sailing world.

After Turner's expulsion from college, he eventually moved to Charleston and took a job with one of his father's billboard companies. While there, he seized the opportunity to be part of Charleston's active and prestigious sailing community, joined the Charleston Harbor Yacht Club, and continued to hone his sailing skills.

From Charleston, Turner headed back to the waters where he had learned to sail as a boy, entered the Y- Flyer National sailing race in Savannah, and won first place. After Turner's victory, his relationship with McIntosh changed. He was no longer a student, casual racing opponent, or just family friend. He was a serious competitor.

A July 2, 1962, newspaper clipping shows the results of the annual 4th of July Regatta held on the Wilmington River. During day one of the two-day event, local skippers taking the lead among the 118 entries were John McIntosh, Tommy Webster, Joe Caldwell, and Teddy Turner.

By the next day, the verdict was in. John McIntosh, Tommy Webster, and Joe Caldwell paced the field in the Lighting, Penguin, and Shark division. Turner, however, lost the Y-Flyer division by a quarter point.

The last time McIntosh sailed against Turner was in the 1965 Senior Y-Flyer National Championship.

"I placed fifth," said McIntosh, with a gleam in his eye, " but Teddy placed sixth."

After Ed Turner's suicide in 1963, Ted took the helm of his father's beleaguered billboard business, determined to turn it around. By 1970, he had not only stabilized the family business but ventured into new areas, purchasing Channel 17 in Atlanta, a foundering UHF station. In six years it became WTBS, the nation's first super station. The same year he bought the Atlanta Braves, eventually turning them into a perennial winner.

As Turner's ambitions soared, so did the propensity for his mouth to get him into trouble. He soon became known as Captain Outrageous and the Mouth of the South. Not that he seemed to care. He was known to have showed up for corporate negotiations decked out in a Confederate officer's uniform, replete with sword and sash, and even challenged fellow media mogul Rupert Murdoch to a televised boxing match in Las Vegas when the two exchanged heated words.

Turner didn't limit his considerable energies to the business world after he left Savannah, but continued to sail as well. He began ocean racing on 40-foot yachts. He bought a Cal-40 named the *Vamp X,* and with a seven-man crew won the Southern Ocean Racing Circuit (SORC) in 1966. He also won the World Ocean Racing Cup in Australia in 1971 by the largest margin in that race's history.

He sailed in the 1974 America's Cup trials, but was eliminated early. The year 1977, however, would prove a different story. He chartered the *Courageous,* made a few modifications, won the trials, and captured the Cup, edging out the *Australia.*

Turner was the last amateur skipper to win the Cup. Now the captains that take the helms of the yachts each year are all paid professionals.

Through the years, McIntosh would occasionally see his old sailing friend, particularly when he was in Atlanta. Often they would lunch together at One CNN Tower or catch a Braves game together. Since 1996, however, when Turner merged his media empire with Time Warner and moved his offices to New York, McIntosh hasn't seen his old sailing buddy.

McIntosh, for his part, continues to teach area youth the basics of sailing at the Savannah Sailing Center at Lake Mayer. And Turner continues to show the same fierce determination, competitiveness, and tenacity in the corporate world that made him such a force to be reckoned with on the water.

Rousakis Ousts Lewis,
A New Political Era Begins

"I'm very much interested in Savannah. I was born and raised here. I'd like to help correct any problems we may have."

With these words John P. Rousakis, a young insurance agent and Chatham County commissioner, officially tossed his hat into the 1970 Savannah mayoral campaign. But before Rousakis could challenge incumbent mayor J.C. Lewis, he had a Democratic opponent to contend with.

Rousakis would face Frank Downing in the Democratic primary. Downing, a native Savannahian and attorney, fell quickly, however, in the May 12 runoff. In light voter turnout, Rousakis swept Downing aside by a margin of two to one, receiving 10,918 votes to Downing's 4,189. Capturing all but five of fifty-six voting boxes, Rousakis received his greatest support from predominately black precincts. In the largely black Eighth District, he beat Downing by more than three to one.

Rousakis' six-alderman slate won over the Democratic opposition as well. Included in the Rousakis sweep was Frank P. Rossiter, Leo Center, F.M. "Woody" Chambers, B.C. Ford, H.C. "Nippie" Morrison, and C. Esbey Thompson

After turning back the opposition in his own party, the Rousakis ticket turned its gaze toward the Lewis administration.

Lewis was an enigma of sorts. First elected as mayor in 1966, he won in a backlash of anti-civil rights sentiment hurled against incumbent Mayor Malcom Maclean. Yet Lewis was no racist. He also promoted progressive legislation, but with less fallout. The Lewis administration, however, was not without its problems.

Lewis, a wealthy Savannah businessman and heir to the Lewis automobile businesses and dealerships, spent little time at City Hall and to many seemed disinterested in his role as mayor, a fact that didn't escape his political foes. Just months prior to the election he remained uncommitted in his reelection plans.

THE ISSUES

While Lewis lurked in the political shadows, Rousakis took to the streets, meeting with groups both large and small. Speaking before a gathering of Savannah Jaycees, Rousakis sought racial conciliation.

"Now our community cries out for harmony and dedicated leadership," he said, "leadership that will pick up the pieces of disunity and mold them with all the great assets and the great talents that we possess in this great city of ours into a united and positive program for a better Savannah."

While Rousakis called for racial harmony, he advocated greater participation of black citizens in city government. This didn't sit well, however, with many white voters, and Rousakis quickly earned political enemies.

Rousakis also challenged the decision of the Lewis administration to charge a 24½ percent water surcharge to pay for the city's pollution abatement program and called for a revamping of the program.

When a citizen's committee recommended that the mayor call for a study to determine how pollution abatement costs could be shared with the county, Lewis merely replied, "No comment." He did state, however, that he would suggest sitting down together to talk with the committee after the election.

The possibility of city-county consolidation also raised passions that election year, dividing many.

Leveling a charge against the Lewis administration, Rousakis insisted that "it was standard procedure for elected officials to step down when faced with city-county consolidation."

Lewis responded by announcing that he and his aldermen would run for reelection to head the consolidated government if and when it was formulated.

Taking the initiative, Rousakis outlined an aggressive annexation plan. He called for legislation to annex areas immediately adjacent to the city limits. Rousakis said that if elected, he could have the annexation proposal drawn up in time to allow the 1971 Georgia General Assembly to consider setting up a referendum to vote on the proposal. He also advocated the sharing of certain city and county services.

Of course, annexation proponents saw increased revenue for every yard of county land brought into the city while opponents resented the incursion of City Hall.

As the election entered its final stretch in July, Rousakis blasted

Lewis, stating that the mayor wasn't even interested in reelection. Speaking before members of the National Maritime Union, Rousakis said he would attempt to expedite the construction of Interstate 16, the Westside Bypass, and Interstate 95 to enhance port activities.

August 4, 1970: The first trickle of Savannah voters entered the polls to cast their vote. By day's end, the Rousakis ticket had made a clean sweep, and the Democratic Party regained control of City Hall. With more than 26,000 votes cast, Rousakis ousted Lewis 14,556 to 11,855. All six aldermen on the Democratic ticket defeated their Republican counterparts. History was also made that day when Bowles C. Ford became the first black to be elected to city office since Reconstruction.

Lewis would settle quietly back into private life, something that most thought he really wanted to do in the first place. Rousakis, however, had just begun.

The native-born son of Greek immigrants would serve as Savannah mayor an unprecedented five terms, from 1970 to 1991. Some of the political pundits to cast their lot against the longtime mayor included Roy Jackson and John Calhoun.

Despite his succession of victories, however, the 1970 election was special to Rousakis. During an interview shortly before his death, he called Lewis a fine man and declared that the 1970 election was one of the cleanest the city had ever seen.

He should have known. He battled the best of them, earning his place in the hearts and minds of generations of Savannahians.

Getting Away with Murder:
A 100-Year-Old Homicide

O n a frigid Saturday evening just before midnight on November 16, 1901, sixty-two-year-old Samuel T. Baker lay dying in a pool of blood in a dark corner of Colonial Cemetery in Savannah. His attackers, whoever they happened to be, were about to get away with murder. As Baker gasped for air, three youths passing by heard him groan.

Leaving his two companions behind with Baker, G.A. Price ran for help. With the police barracks within shouting distance, he didn't have to run far. He returned with two Savannah patrolmen, Lawrence J. Dwyer and John J. Farrell. After quickly sizing up the situation, the officers carried Baker to the barracks and booked him on charges of intoxication.

But Baker wasn't drunk. He'd been the victim of a heinous crime, one that has confounded friends and family members for 100 years.

"Samuel Baker was likely killed by a Savannah policeman," said Cynthia Jacobson, Baker's great-great-granddaughter. Jacobson learned the story from her grandmother, Marie Hopkins Steadman. Steadman was only one year old when her grandfather was assaulted, but the details of the murder stayed etched in her mind until her death in 1999 at ninety-eight years of age.

"Grandma told me that Samuel had been murdered by a Savannah police officer," Jacobson said. "Not only was he murdered, but it was a cover up, that is until the officer died."

The officer confessed the crime shortly before his death, according to Mrs. Steadman. But Jacobson never asked her grandmother for the officer's name, and when she died she took it to her grave.

Now, a century after his death, and without her grandmother's help, Jacobson seeks justice for her great-great-grandfather.

But solving a 100-year-old murder isn't easy, particularly if it might have been a police homicide.

Death certificates, vital statistics, and newspaper accounts are readily available, but the Savannah Police Department didn't keep internal affairs records in 1901, making the task more difficult.

Samuel T. Baker. (Photo from the author's collection)

PIECING TOGETHER THE DETAILS

To try to find Baker's killer, then, is to retrace his steps the fateful night of his murder.

Baker, a bookkeeper for John Lynes & Company, had collected money for his employer for most of the day. As was his custom, he returned to the shop to deposit the funds. He also drew a dollar of his salary.

After leaving his office, Baker walked to Gayou's Barber Shop on Broughton Street for a shave, probably for the morning service at Independent Presbyterian Church, where he was a member.

Before Baker left the store, however, he spoke briefly with his son-in-law E.M. Hopkins a few minutes before eleven. After the conversation, Hopkins left for his 416 Charlton Street home, where he, his wife, and children lived with Mr. and Mrs. Baker.

From Gayou's Barber Shop, Baker walked home, crossing State, President, and York streets. From York he crossed Oglethorpe Avenue, then took his usual shortcut through Colonial Cemetery. Within shouting distance of the police barracks, in the southwest corner of the cemetery, two men attacked Baker. With walking stick in hand, Baker fought back. He was struck twice in the head with a blunt object and collapsed. As he fell, a bottle of liquor, bought for an ailing relative, crashed with him, leaking its contents into the ground.

After Baker was found by Price, Harry Ferris, and Thomas McDonnell at approximately 12:30 A.M. and then booked on intoxication charges by officers Dwyer and Farrell, police surgeon Dr. Elton Osborne was summoned. A quick examination by Osborne revealed a fractured skull, two black eyes, and several cuts and bruises on the face. Baker's delirious speech, presumed by Dwyer and Farrell to be drunken mutterings, proved to be a by-product of the wounds. According to Osborne, Baker had been the victim of a violent assault.

Missing were Baker's watch and chain, and a set of keys—including keys to John Lynes & Company. The only money Baker had on him, 72 cents, remained untouched in his coat pocket. His trouser pants pockets were turned inside out and his walking stick lay nearby, covered in blood.

As Baker sat in a semi-conscious state at the police barracks, Hopkins worried elsewhere.

Around two o'clock in the morning, Hopkins set out on foot to try to find his father-in-law. Tracing Baker's usual route, Hopkins cut through Colonial Cemetery, where he passed a pool of blood. Sensing the worst, he hurried to Baker's place of employment, hoping to find him working on the books later than usual.

When Hopkins reached the shop, he spoke with a fruit vendor on the corner who confirmed that Baker left just after eleven to go to the barbershop for a shave. Hopkins rushed from the store to the police barracks, where his worst fears were confirmed.

After carrying Baker home, Hopkins tried to help his father-in-law undress and prepare him for bed. Baker resisted.

"Don't do that," he muttered. "Leave my clothes and shoes. There are two to one, please leave my clothing."

Hopkins pressed for more information about the attack, but in vain. All he could surmise from Baker's mutterings were that there were two assailants. Though attended by physicians, Baker struggled for several hours before slipping away forever. At six that evening he died.

News of Baker's death hit Savannah hard. As his family prepared to bury him, police thought they had a lead.

One of Baker's relatives informed police that Baker had had a confrontation several weeks earlier in the cemetery. While Baker walked home from work through the park, a man had jumped out and challenged him. But Baker raised his walking stick ready to attack and the man moved aside and let him pass.

"He laughed at the fear," said the family member, "and said it would probably never happen again."

As police detectives tried to follow leads, theories about Baker's murder emerged from all corners. One theory implied that the robbers, knowing of Baker's large collection of funds earlier in the day, lay in wait, hoping that Baker would carry the money with him on his way home. Police quickly dismissed that theory, however, because it was thought that those with the knowledge that Baker had a large sum of money would have also known that he always deposited the money before walking home.

Another theory suggested that Baker, walking home alone at night, encountered a trio of drunken men. Supposedly, they spotted the bottle of liquor under Baker's arm and made a dash for it. Baker resisted, was struck in the head, and fell to the ground.

The bruises and cuts on his face may have been the result of being struck by a fist before falling to the ground. After Baker fell, he could have been kicked in the head, resulting in a fractured skull. Since his walking stick was covered with blood, it was thought that Baker had put up a fight.

A more plausible explanation of Baker's murder suggested that Baker was robbed for the keys to the store. Because no one sought to use the keys and nothing was missing from the store, this theory, too, was later dismissed. Soon after, Mr. Lynes changed the locks on the store doors.

The local press favored the idea that Baker wasn't robbed, but was mistaken for someone else, and attacked. Once the assailants discovered their mistake, it was claimed, they made the attack look like a robbery.

While theories came and went, friends and family members paid their last respects.

The day after Baker's murder, the *Savannah Press* reported, "He did not have an enemy in the world, as he was one of the most genial and social men in the city. He was kind and charitable, with a smile and a word of cheer for everybody."

BAKER'S WAR RECORD

The Charlton Street native had moved to Savannah shortly after the end of the Civil War and took a job as a bookkeeper for John Lynes & Company, married, and fathered two children. Baker also authored two volumes of poetry, *Fort Sumter and its Defenders* and *Fort Sumter: Its Hero and Reward,* both of which drew on his wartime experiences.

Shortly after South Carolina opened fire on Federal troops at Fort Sumter on April 12, 1861, twenty-two-year-old Samuel T. Baker enlisted in the 9th South Carolina Volunteer Regiment, Company A, as a private. Eager to taste war, the unit took up positions guarding the coastal approaches to Beaufort County.

In November 1861, Baker's unit joined troops garrisoned at Fort Beauregard at Hilton Head in an attempt to hold off a Federal naval attack at Port Royal Sound. Though determined, the Southern troops were largely untrained, undermanned, and short of ammunition—simply no match for the seventy-five-ship U.S. Navy armada facing them.

After Federal warships fired broadsides at the fort, gunboats finished the job, disabling the remaining Confederate guns. At 2 P.M. on November 7, Confederate troops abandoned the fort. Across the bay, Fort Walker also capitulated and Hilton Head fell. It remained in Federal hands for the balance of the war.

On March 14, 1862, Company A reorganized as an independent artillery unit and was designated Captain H.M. Stuart's Company, Beaufort Volunteer Artillery.

The Beaufort Volunteer Artillery spent the next two years on costal patrol in and around Charleston. During a firefight with blockading ships on April 9, 1863, they destroyed the *USS George Washington*. The unit also skirmished with Federal infantry on several occasions. In addition to manning the guns during this two-year period, Baker performed clerical work, serving four different stints as clerk for the court martial section of the military department of South Carolina, Georgia, and Florida.

When Northern troops threatened to seize Savannah in late 1864, the Beaufort Volunteer Artillery was attached to Gen. Lafayette McLaw's division in defense of the city. On November 30, the unit linked forces with approximately 1,400 Georgia state militia in fighting at Honey Hill (Jasper County), South Carolina. They successfully repulsed a force of Union regulars three times their strength seeking to cut the Charleston & Savannah Railroad.

After Savannah fell on December 20, 1864, the Beaufort Volunteer Artillery swung into South Carolina and joined Gen. Joseph E. Johnston's ragtag force of 20,000 in a futile attempt to stop Sherman's 60,000-man thrust through the Carolinas. The unit surrendered as part of Johnston's army in North Carolina on April 26, 1865.

Writing of the vanquished South in *Fort Sumter and its Defenders,* Baker penned:

> Her heart is broken; like a statue now
> With form erect, the Cypress round her brow,
> Her bare arm lifted, and her finger tip
> Is placed in sadness on her silent lip.

Wrapped in Confederate colors, Baker's remains were interred at Laurel Grove Cemetery on Tuesday afternoon, November 18. As family members filed out of the cemetery, most wondered if they would ever find Baker's killer.

On November 20, two days after Baker was buried, the *Morning News* reported, "Police Have A Clue: Colonial Park Murder May Be Solved Soon."

A bundle of clothing had been found in the cemetery near where

Baker was attacked. While detectives sought to unravel the mystery, many pointed fingers at the police department.

Some claimed that a patrolman making his way through the park struck Baker in the head. After recognizing his mistake, the officer panicked and turned Baker's trouser pockets inside out, removed his watch, chain, and keys, and arranged the scene to resemble a robbery. If true, the theory would help explain why Baker still had money in his coat pocket when found by patrolmen Dwyer and Farrell. Angered over Baker's intoxication booking, others sought a police inquiry.

Mayor Herman Myers, however, defended the actions of the police department.

"The police are to blame in only one particular," he said. "That was entering a charge of drunkenness against Mr. Baker. In every other way they acted in a proper manner."

Despite the mayor's defense, lingering questions remained.

Why did officers Dwyer and Farrell book Baker on intoxication charges when he was obviously gravely injured and no signs of alcohol consumption were found? The police surgeon and the three men who found Baker confirmed the severity of Baker's injuries. In a *Morning News* interview, Price, Ferris, and McDonnell affirmed that they immediately recognized the seriousness of Baker's wounds and that they were likely the result of an assault, not of a drunken fall.

In addition, a fall could not have inflicted such heavy blows on the top part of the skull. Did Dwyer and Farrell book Baker to cover for a fellow officer's indiscretion?

Furthermore, the assault took place in Colonial Cemetery, within shouting distance of the police barracks. Why didn't police hear the commotion?

Finally, did an officer attack Baker, return to headquarters, and then enlist the help of Dwyer and Farrell?

On the 21st, J.N. Baker, Baker's nephew, arrived in town from Beaufort to push the investigation.

Critical of the way police were handling leads, Baker suggested that his uncle had been lying wounded in the cemetery for an hour before he was found and could have been robbed by thieves after the assault.

The same day the *Evening Press* reported that a number of citizens were pressing both city and county governments to offer a reward leading to the arrest of Baker's murderers. Some also believed that if two or more men committed the crime, one would turn state's evidence to avoid a murder prosecution.

Adding to the suspicion, the coroner's report concluded that Baker's head wound had been inflicted by a blunt object, possibly a billy-club or the butt of a revolver. Coroner Keller argued that Baker's injuries could not have been caused by a fall and confirmed that Baker had been murdered.

The coroner's report added credence to the Baker family claim that Samuel had been assaulted by a police officer, particularly since officers often patrolled the streets with billy-clubs in hand.

Experts state that a homicide committed with a blunt object can be premeditated, but is usually one of impulse and is often the result of sudden fury or sometimes surprise or fear. For example, a burglar breaks into a house and batters the homeowner he has inadvertently awakened. A blow to the head is also one of the most inefficient methods of murder, and it often takes repeated blows to kill the intended victim. A heavy blow to the head causes tissue laceration, and if heavy enough, a fractured skull—the same way Baker had been killed.

MURDERER NEVER APPREHENDED

Yet, Baker's murderer was never found. Shortly after he was buried, police dropped the investigation. It wasn't until years later, according to Baker's family, that the officer who killed Baker made a deathbed confession.

"As far as I'm concerned Samuel T. Baker was murdered by mistake, unknowingly, by a police officer," said Betty Burks, Baker's great-granddaughter.

Cynthia Jacobson agrees, but added, "My grandmother knew the officer's name. We should have found out before she died. Maybe someone who reads the story will remember hearing about it years ago and come forward."

If the two arresting officers, Dwyer and Farrell, made a deathbed confession, it didn't make the papers. A check of both men's obituaries reveals little more than their dates and places of birth and where they were buried. It is probable, however, that Dwyer and Farrell found Baker, but had nothing to do with his killing. They merely responded to a call in the early morning hours on November 17, 1901.

If another officer did, indeed, kill Baker, it may be impossible to prove. Not only have 100 years lapsed, but uncovering a homicide committed by a police officer is always difficult.

Officer Vance McLaughlin of the Savannah Police Department came across references to Baker's murder while conducting research for a book, *100 Years of Homicide in Savannah.* But he found little more than newspaper clippings.

"No one was ever caught for the murder," he said, "but it was a strange one for two reasons. It occurred right by the police barracks, and also it was rare not to find the murderer of a white male back then."

Baker's family remains convinced of the story handed down to them.

"We don't think that the Savannah Police Department was necessarily involved in Baker's murder or was even involved in a cover up," said Jacobson. "We do think though that one of their officers blundered by striking Samuel, then panicked and tried to cover up his mistake. He didn't want to take it to his grave, so he made a deathbed confession."

Perhaps Baker's murderer may never be found. Perhaps he was slain by a police officer or killed in a robbery gone bad.

"Even if we never find Sam's killer," said Jacobson, "at least his story and the facts are finally out. And with that—there is a certain justice."

PART TWO:
The Personalities

James Pierpont,
Expatriate, Rebel, Composer

James Pierpont led an interesting and uncontroversial life. Born in New England in 1822 to John Pierpont, an abolitionist and Unitarian clergyman, he traveled to Savannah in the 1850s, wrote the timeless classic "Jingle Bells," and took up arms against his native state during the Civil War.

When little James was born, John Pierpont had little reason to suspect that his son would rebel so ardently and so long. James ran away from home at the tender age of fourteen, boarded the *Shark,* and served as a deck hand in the Pacific. Eventually returning, he headed to California during the Gold Rush.

In 1846, James was back in New England, where he married Millicent Cowee of Troy, New York. They settled in Medford, Massachusetts, and had three children. In 1853, Millicent died prematurely and James headed to Savannah to visit his brother John Pierpont, Jr., rector of the Unitarian Church at Troup Square. Eventually taking the position of music director, James tried to piece his life back together. In 1857, he married Eliza Jane Purse, daughter of wartime Savannah mayor Thomas Purse. The same year he obtained a copyright for his song "The One-Horse Open Sleigh," which later became "Jingle Bells."

Apparently James' father-in-law had a significant impact on him. James saw hypocrisy in the North's anti-slavery stance, since many Northern fortunes had been made from it. In April 1862, James enlisted as a clerk in the Lamar Rangers, an elite cavalry unit, which soon became part of the 5th Georgia Volunteer Cavalry.

True to form, his father accepted a position as a chaplain in the Union Army and served with the 22nd Massachusetts Volunteers.

Later he worked in the Treasury Department and became friends with the Lincoln family. He died soon after the war.

It is likely that James saw limited action during his war years. Few traces are left of his military record. However, an 1863 Savannah newspaper ad offered a reward for a stolen horse that belonged to "James Pierpont of the Isle of Hope Regiment."

James composed several patriotic songs during his war years, including "We Conquer or Die," "Our Battle Flag," and "Strike for the South."

After the war, James spent time in Valdosta and Quitman and eventually became a music professor at Quitman Academy. His last years were spent at his son's home in Winter Haven, Florida. In spite of his song's eventual success, James never witnessed the enormous popularity of "Jingle Bells," enjoying neither fame nor fortune. He died in 1893 as a footnote in history, his accomplishments largely unrecognized. He was buried in Florida, but was re-interred less than a year later at Laurel Grove Cemetery in Savannah.

"JINGLE BELLS" CONTROVERSY

A controversy erupted in 1989 when the people of Medford, Massachusetts, claimed that James had written "Jingle Bells" there and not in Savannah. Medford mayor Michael J. McGlynn fired the first shot. In a letter to then-Savannah mayor John P. Rousakis, he states: "We take strong exception to Mr. Rahn's theory that 'Jingle Bells' was not written in Medford, Mass. in 1850."

McGlynn's claims are based on two things: a historical marker that once stood in front of the Simpson Tavern where James supposedly composed the song, and an eyewitness. The marker was damaged by a snowplow and discarded, but the Medford Historical Society has a record of the marker. According to McGlynn, the marker is proof of his city's claims. In addition, McGlynn states that Pierpont composed "Jingle Bells" in front of a witness, a Mrs. Otis Waterman, "at the Simpson Tavern on Mr. William Weber's piano in 1850!"

On May 24, Rousakis replied: "We are happy to share with you our documentation regarding James Lord Pierpont's years in

Savannah." Rousakis cites numerous Pierpont letters to disprove the Medford theory. "As you know," Rousakis wrote, "historians and those who propose to erect markers must work with facts, not folklore and assumptions." Rousakis lists several reasons to substantiate his own claims.

Local author Margaret DeBolt, who has studied and written extensively about Pierpont, sees holes in McGlynn's theory. "In 1850 Pierpont was in California, not in Medford," she said. "He was there during the Gold Rush, not as a miner but as a businessman, and was also trying to set up a photography shop in San Francisco.

"Plus," she adds, "the Simpson Tavern referred to was a boarding house in 1850. Only later did it become a tavern."

The controversy remains and both cities have markers that claim Pierpont's song as their own. Yet, a few facts are constant: Both agree that the song originated from Pierpont's remembrance of his childhood days spent sleighing in the New England snow, and "Jingle Bells," no matter where it was written, has been a holiday favorite for over a century.

Conrad Aiken,
Prize-Winning Poet Laureate

In the early morning hours of February 28, 1901, eleven-year-old Conrad Aiken burst through the doors of his home and ran into the streets. Noticing a policeman walking a beat, young Aiken mustered his courage.

"My mama and papa are dead," he said. "I just found them. Papa shot mama and shot himself."

In the Aiken home on Oglethorpe Avenue, both parents lay dead, his mother on her bed and his father next to her on the floor. Aiken's father, Dr. William Ford Aiken, had shot his wife in the head, then turned the gun on himself. They left four small children..

Conrad's father was a young and prominent Savannah physician who had established himself not only locally, but also statewide.

His mother, an intelligent, kind woman, was a good wife and devoted mother. What went wrong?

Rumors spread. The most prevalent theory was that the Aiken family had a long history of mental illness. Conrad's father lived in constant dread of suffering a similar fate, so he killed himself. Another rumor implied that Mrs. Aiken believed her husband was insane and planned to commit him to an insane asylum. In an attempt to avoid the inevitable, he ended his life.

After their parents' death, the Aiken children were separated. Conrad traveled to New Bedford, Massachusetts, to live with a great-aunt, while the other children were sent to various relatives in the South.

Having heard the gunshots and finding his parents' lifeless bodies would haunt Aiken for the rest of his life. He would spend years trying to come to terms with the trauma, developing a keen interest in psychoanalysis.

Years later, reflecting upon that horrid moment, he wrote: "Finding them dead, I found myself possessed of them forever."

Aiken entered Yale University and became friends with future Nobel Prize-winner T.S. Eliot, who was at the school for just a couple of months. After graduating in 1912, Aiken worked as a reporter for a short time, but quit to devote his full attention to creative writing. In 1914, Aiken's first collection of poems, *Earth Triumphant,* was published.

When World War I broke out, Aiken applied for a military exemption, claiming that his writing was an "essential industry." Surprisingly, the U.S. Army agreed, and Aiken was spared the horrors of war.

During the most prolific period of his writing career, from the 1920s to the 1950s, Aiken divided his time between England and the States. In 1924, he edited Emily Dickinson's *Selected Poems.* This volume was largely responsible for establishing her literary fame posthumously. In the 1920s and 1930s, Aiken turned out a series of novels: *Blue Voyage, King Coffin, Among Lost People, Bring! Bring!,* and *Great Circle.*

KINDRED SPIRITS

Freud's psychoanalytical theories were emerging at the time, and Aiken found them intriguing. He based much of his work on these ideas. In return, Freud considered Aiken's writings, particularly his *Great Circle,* masterpieces of analytical introspection.

Aiken won a Pulitzer Prize in 1930 for a collection of poems. His poetry, which is often preoccupied with the sound and structure of music, can be haunting. The first stanza of "Music I Heard" is one of the great love lyrics of all time:

Music I heard with you was more than music,
and bread I broke with you was more than bread.
Now that I am without you, all is desolate:
all that was once so beautiful is dead.

Aiken wrote his autobiographic *Ushant* in 1952. In it he describes his happy, carefree days growing up in Savannah. While his father worked and his mother took care of the other Aiken children, Conrad wandered the streets of Savannah. Roaming the waterfront, he would watch tall ships sail up the Savannah River and spend hours gazing at the sea gulls along the river.

In *Ushant,* some of these early scenes are described: his "inescapable mother; the sea," "the tall shuttered windows of his three story house with its brick stoop and iron railing," and the "rich dirt of the Savannah streets."

In 1962, Aiken began wintering in Savannah in an Oglethorpe Avenue house, adjacent to the site where his parents had been killed. He spent most of the remainder of his life there, reflecting and writing.

In an interview with the *New York Times* on his eightieth birthday, Aiken complained that his work had not received just recognition and that he was never understood. If so, he has become better understood in the years since his death. Yet many claim that he is still a largely unappreciated figure in American literature.

Aiken's last poem, "Thee," was written in 1971 and published in 1973. In April 1973, Georgia Gov. Jimmy Carter granted Aiken the honorary position of state poet laureate. Aiken died six months later and was buried in Bonaventure Cemetery.

Gen. James Oglethorpe, Georgia's Founder

Gen. James Oglethorpe is known as the founder of Georgia, but his life extended far beyond that one accomplishment. He was an English patriot who often challenged the status quo, a politician, a soldier, a humanitarian, and philanthropist.

Born into an aristocratic family in London on December 22, 1696, James was the son of Theophilus and Eleanor Oglethorpe, both ardent Jacobites loyal to the House of Stuart. Yet young James would form his own ideas and prove to be not only an aristocrat but one with a heart.

In 1715, at the age of nineteen, James secured a commission in His Majesty's army, but within two years migrated to Paris. He joined the army that served under Prince Eugene of Savoy, the victor over the Ottoman Turks at Belgrade.

After returning to England, James ran for Parliament in 1722 and served for thirty-two years as a mild High Tory, occupying the seat previously held by his father and two older brothers. In 1731, Oglethorpe finished his studies at Eton College and Corpus Christi College, Oxford, earning a master's degree.

HIGH IDEALS

In Parliament, James advocated equality for all subjects of the British Empire, criticized royal extravagances, opposed slavery, and pushed for prison reform. After being appointed to a committee to study prison conditions, he wrote *The Sailor's Advocayte,* exposing the evils of the English penal system. The book, originally published in 1732, went through eight printings and proved to be the turning point in his political career.

From these ideals came James' impetus to found a new colony where newly freed and unemployed debtors could find a new start. Lobbying intensely for his cause, he began to attract funds. Yet, it is likely that his vision for a new colony would never have materialized were it not for military necessity.

South Carolina, the southern frontier of the British Empire in

James Oglethorpe monument in Chippewa Square. (Photo
courtesy Henderson Studios, Savannah)

North America, was constantly being raided by the Spanish from their bases in Florida. In an effort to remedy the problem, a buffer state was called for. This need coincided with Oglethorpe's mission, and on June 8, 1732, Oglethorpe and nineteen associates were granted a charter and appointed as trustees for a new colony to be called Georgia, named for King George II.

After a three-month voyage across the Atlantic, the ship *Anne* made port at Charleston to secure supplies. Sailing up the Savannah River, Oglethorpe and 114 immigrants finally landed at Yamacraw Bluff on February 12, 1733, and the last of the thirteen original colonies was founded.

The newcomers immediately began negotiations with the local Indians. The first and most famous meeting was with Tomochichi, chief of the Yamacraw tribe. Not being able to convince them to form a military alliance, Oglethorpe nevertheless was successful in persuading them to discontinue communications with the French and Spanish and sign a treaty of neutrality.

OGLETHORPE'S PROHIBITIONS

Oglethorpe, a staunch moralist, quickly established a list of prohibitions: no rum, brandies, or strong spirits; no lawyers and no slavery. In addition, open papal worship was prohibited. Though harsh, the edict against Catholicism served to prevent large gatherings of Catholics, who were thought to be supporters of Roman Catholic Spain.

Writing about slavery, Oglethorpe said: "If we allow slaves we act against the very principles by which we associated together, which was to relieve the distressed." But the slavery ban soon became unpopular and within a few years was repealed.

In the ensuing years, Oglethorpe traveled between England and the colonies several times. He first returned to England in 1734, accompanied by Tomochichi, to secure funds and revive interest in the new colony. But rumors of insurrection brought him back in 1735, accompanied by two young clergymen destined to set the religious world on end—John and Charles Wesley.

Twice Oglethorpe led unsuccessful invasions against the Spanish in St. Augustine. In fact, he was severely criticized at the time for his over-involvement in military affairs and his neglect of administrative duties. Consequently, many called for his resignation. He was successful, however, in defending Georgia against Spanish incursions, particularly in his victory at the battle of Bloody Marsh. Soon after Bloody Marsh the Spanish threat to the southern colonies all but ceased.

After Oglethorpe's last Florida invasion in 1743, one of his subordinates brought charges against him. He returned to England to face a court martial, and the charges were dropped. But the cost was his colonial career. He would never set foot again in Georgia.

Oglethorpe spent the rest of his long life in and around London, finally marrying at the age of forty-seven. He did, however, fight in the Seven Years' War (1756-1762) in Europe under an assumed name.

Retaining an interest in Georgia and the southern colonies, Oglethorpe spoke out on their behalf during the American Revolution. Though aged, he lived long enough to see the colonies gain their independence and in 1785 called on John Adams, the first U.S. minister to England. Oglethorpe died on June 30 of the same year. His statue, in full military attire, stands guard in Chippewa Square in Savannah facing southward toward Florida and his colonial enemies.

Gen. Nathanael Greene, Victim of a Hot Savannah Summer

Savannah's summers are hot, an accepted fact. But for Revolutionary War hero Nathanael Greene, the summers were too hot.

Shortly after the end of the war, Greene, a war hero and confidant of Gen. George Washington, was rewarded for helping drive the British army out of Georgia. In 1785, the Georgia Legislature gave him 5,000 guineas. Later that same year he was given title to Mulberry Grove Plantation, twelve miles east of Savannah. The plantation had recently been confiscated from former Loyalist Lieutenant Governor Graham. Initially, silk was grown on the plantation, but without success. Rice and cotton became the primary cash crop.

Greene despised Savannah's summer heat, and the story is told, at least by some local historians, of how Greene would walk in his fields every morning wearing a wide-brimmed hat for protection from the sun. Some even claim he had a thermometer hanging from the brim to monitor the heat. One hot June afternoon in 1786, Greene ventured into a rice field without his hat. He suffered a heat stroke and died. He was only forty-four.

Greene left a wife, Caty, and five children. After the general's death, Caty ran into financial trouble. Greene had spent most of his fortune to help support the war effort, and little remained. In 1792, with George Washington's help, Caty persuaded Congress to grant her $47,000.

It was at Mulberry Grove that a young Eli Whitney, not long out of Yale, designed the cotton gin and turned the South's economy upside down.

PREPARING FOR WAR

Nathanael worked at his father's iron foundry in Potowomut (Warwick), Rhode Island, until 1770. The same year, the twenty-nine-year-old built a home at Coventry to take care of another family forge. Between 1770 and 1772 and again in 1775 Greene served as deputy of the state General Assembly. He became interested in the military and joined a local militia unit, the Kentish Guards. Having little formal education or military training, he read widely and versed himself in military science and tactics.

On April 19, 1775, the first formal engagement of the Revolution erupted. A force of 700 British regulars marched toward Concord to confiscate colonial military supplies. In their path stood only seventy Minutemen. By the end of the engagement, eight Colonials lay dead and ten were wounded.

When news of the fighting at Lexington reached Rhode Island, the Kentish Guards proceeded to Massachusetts, but were recalled by Rhode Island's loyalist governor. Not to be deterred, Greene, still a private, and three others marched on to Boston to join the fight for independence.

In May, the Rhode Island General Assembly voted to raise three regiments for the war effort and appointed Greene as brigadier general. The same month he marched his unit to Cambridge, where it became part of the Continental Army. There he met George Washington, with whom he later became a close friend and one of his most trusted aides.

Greene served conspicuously on the battlefield during the war's darkest hours. Constantly outnumbered, he earned a reputation as a skilled fighter. He was with Washington at the historic crossing of the Delaware River. That horrible winter at Valley Forge when the Continental army—hungry, cold, and destitute—almost ceased to exist, Greene was there at Washington's side.

Toward war's end, when the fighting shifted to the south, Greene found an army without discipline, arms, or clothing. Within a year, he had forged a formidable fighting force and helped bring the war to a conclusion. Unfortunately, a few years later he was dead. His funeral was described as one with much "pomp and fanfare." With the Chatham Artillery officiating, he was buried at the Colonial Cemetery in Savannah.

LOOKING FOR GENERAL GREENE

In spite of his fame, the exact location of Greene's grave soon became a mystery. In 1819, the Savannah City Council tried to locate his remains, without success. Almost a century later, in 1901, the Rhode Island State Society of the Cincinnati resumed the task. After a long and exhausting search, Greene's remains were finally identified. The general's bones and those of his son, George Washington Greene, were placed in a zinc-lined box and secured in a vault at the Southern Bank.

After much debate, a decision was made to re-inter Greene's remains at the base of the Greene Monument on Johnson Square. Finally, the warrior-patriot could rest.

G. Moxley Sorrel:
Staff Officer's Fortunes of War

Described as tall, slender, and graceful, with keen, dark eyes and a military bearing, G. Moxley Sorrel had the opportunity to associate with Confederate generals, Southern politicians, and top officials during the Civil War. He witnessed, first hand, the workings, personality conflicts, and complexities of the Confederate high command.

Sorrel was born in Savannah on February 23, 1838. His grandfather, a colonel of engineers in the French army, moved to the United States after his retirement. The Sorrel family settled in Virginia, and eventually made their way to Georgia. Attending Chatham Academy for a brief period of time, Sorrel received training in military tactics and drill. He grew up in the Francis-Sorrel house on Bull Street.

The year 1860 found young Sorrel working as a clerk in the banking department of the Central of Georgia Railroad and serving as a private in the Georgia Hussars, an elite cavalry unit. But when war between North and South became imminent in 1861, Sorrel shirked his banking duties and slipped away to Charleston to watch the bombardment of Fort Sumter by South Carolina militia.

As part of the Georgia Hussars, Sorrel served two brief tours of duty, one at Skidaway Island and the other during the capture of Fort Pulaski. Despite this, his unit had not yet been officially accepted into the Confederate army. Growing impatient for the Confederate government to recognize his unit and send it to the front lines, Sorrel headed to Virginia, then at the forefront of the conflict. Arriving in Virginia just days before the battle of Bull Run, he became a volunteer aid on Gen. James Longstreet's staff and finally tasted battle. Sorrel's father, who had connections with Confederate Gen. P.G.T. Beauregard, helped his son secure the position.

ARMY OF NORTHERN VIRGINIA

Within a few weeks, Sorrel was named Longstreet's adjutant, and subsequently rose in rank from captain to lieutenant colonel.

Sorrel's fortunes of war paralleled those of Robert E. Lee's famous Army of Northern Virginia. He participated in nearly all of the war's major battles in the East: Manassas (Bull Run), Seven Pines, the Seven Day's battles, Second Manassas, Sharpsburg (Antietam), Fredricksburg, Gettysburg, the Wilderness, Spotsylvania, Cold Harbor, and the Petersburg siege.

He tasted the fruits of victory during the first two years of war as the Army of Northern Virginia smashed their Federal counterparts. During the last two years of the war, he shared the depredations and defeat of a struggling army whose shrinking numbers ensured defeat.

Sorrel served conspicuously in several battles, eventually earning a brigadier general's three stars. At Sharpsburg, when the Confederate center was about to collapse and a column of Federals was advancing, Sorrel and three other staff officers dismounted, manned two pieces of Washington artillery, and held the Federals in check until reinforcements could arrive. This action kept the Confederate line from crumbling, saving Lee's army from annihilation.

As adjutant general of Longstreet's Corps, Sorrel witnessed the carnage at Gettysburg and participated in the surprise Confederate victory at Chickamauga and the subsequent loss at Knoxville.

During the Wilderness battles, Sorrel personally led four brigades against Gen. Winfield Scott Hancock in a successful envelopment of the Union left, earning the praise of Robert E. Lee. At Hatcher's Run, Sorrel was shot through one of his lungs.

The Federals were so confident of his death that the *New York Herald* ran Sorrel's obituary, but Sorrel recuperated. As he did, Lee's army left the trenches and dugouts around Petersburg in an attempt to reach the safety of Danville's hilly terrain. Sorrel was on his way back to his command when he heard of Lee's surrender at Appomattox Court House.

After the war, Sorrel returned to Savannah and served on the city council from June 18, 1873, to September 8, 1875. He was acting vice president of the Georgia Historical Society for twelve years and chairman of the board of managers for Telfair Academy. He became manager of the Ocean Steamship Company and later managed the company's New York office. In 1894, he returned to Savannah and became manager of the Georgia Export and Import Company.

Soon after his return to Savannah, Sorrel became ill and moved to Virginia to be closer to his brother, Dr. Francis Sorrel. Apparently sensing death close at hand, he wrote his memoirs, *The Recollections of a Confederate Staff Officer.*

In the book, he describes with color and detail his war experiences and his privileged glimpse of Confederate war strategy. He died near Roanoke, Virginia, on August 10, 1901. His body was returned to Savannah and buried at Laurel Grove Cemetery.

Flannery O'Connor,
Southern Novelist and Enigma

Of the myriad of writers that the South has produced in the last 100 years, Flannery O'Connor stands out as an enigma. Considered to be an eccentric by many of her peers, her works now claim universal respect and are still being read, studied, and written about more than thirty years after her death.

Flannery was born in Savannah in 1925 to a well-to-do Roman Catholic family. She spent the first fourteen years of her life at the O'Connor home on East Charlton Street, a stone's throw from the Cathedral of St. John the Baptist. After her father died from lupus, Flannery and her mother, Regina Cline O'Connor, returned to the Cline ancestral home in Millidgeville. By all accounts, the Cline home was impressive. The 1820 structure served as the governor's residence for a short period of time when Millidgeville was the state capital.

In Millidgeville, Flannery was raised to be a Southern belle, something she rebelled against. She stated:

> I was in my early days, forced to take dancing to throw me into the company of other children and to make me graceful. Nothing I hated worse than the company of other children and I vowed I'd see them all in hell before I would make the first graceful move.

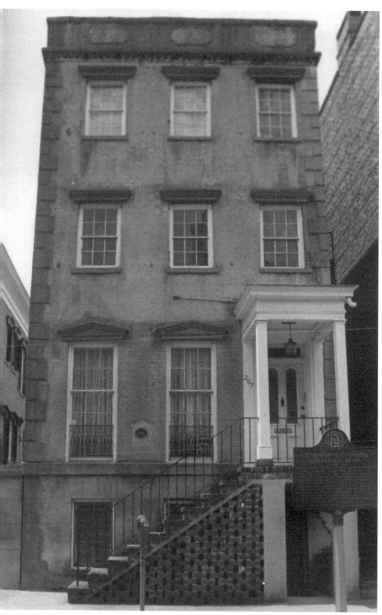

Flannery O'Connor's childhood home on Lafayette Square
in Savannah. (Photo by Karri Cormican)

Flannery graduated from Peabody High School in Millidgeville in 1945 and soon enrolled in Georgia State College for Women (now Georgia College and State University). Majoring in English and sociology, she began to write prolifically.

A WRITER'S APPRENTICE

From 1945 to 1947 Flannery attended the University of Iowa and participated in the school's acclaimed Writer's Workshop. While in Iowa, she published her first short story, "The Geranium," in *Accent* magazine and developed the practice of writing at the same place for a set number of hours each day.

In a 1962 interview, she stated: "I write every day. But often nothing comes of my efforts. They don't lead anywhere. I rewrite, edit, throw away. It's slow and searching. I'm not sure until it's down on paper."

After graduating from the University of Iowa with a master's degree in fine arts, Flannery set off for New York. Like many young writers, she wanted to live and work in what many considered the optimal setting. In fact, Flannery, known for her Southern works, wanted to live anywhere but her native South. She spent nine months in a writing colony in Saratoga Springs, New York, then moved to Manhattan and boarded at the YWCA.

While in New York she met and became friends with Robert Fitzgerald, a noted translator of Homer, and his wife, Sally, who later became Flannery's biographer.

From September 1949 to December 1950 she lived at the Fitzgerald residence in exchange for baby-sitting duties. It was here, in the tranquility of a quiet, upstate country home, that Flannery completed her first novel, *Wise Blood*.

She became ill from lupus, however, and had to spend several months hospitalized in Georgia. Eventually she had to undergo a blood transfusion. This ended the young writer's quest for independence. She had no choice but to return to Millidgeville and her mother's care.

Wise Blood received mixed reviews. In the South it was considered controversial, but it received praise in the North. Many Southerners felt that the book made fun of them and the region.

Wise Blood is written in a Tennessee-Georgia dialect. Its main character, Hazel Mote (a man), grapples with religion in a strange tale of affliction and tormented people.

Yet, this was O'Connor's style. According to many literary critics, she wrote about the two things that were prominent in her life—religion and the South. She viewed the human condition as one of affliction and suffering. Religion was an often ill-fated attempt to make sense of it all.

After her return to Millidgeville, Flannery was forced to walk with crutches, but still kept a busy schedule. Usually writing in the early part of the day, she often painted in the afternoon and spent time with her pet swans and peacocks. She also traveled and frequently lectured at colleges and universities on the subjects of religion and writing.

Her collection of short stories, *A Good Man Is Hard To Find,* was published in 1955, as was another novel, *The Violent Bear It Away.*

In early 1964, she underwent surgery to have removed an abdominal tumor complicating her lupus. By August, she was dead. She was buried at Memory Hill Cemetery next to her father. A second volume of short stories, *Everything That Rises Must Converge,* was published posthumously in 1965.

Mary Telfair, Uncompromising Philanthropist

In the Telfair Museum, among statues and works of art, Mary Telfair's portrait rests on the wall. Her stern gaze, hair piled in a bun, and high-necked blouse add to the aura of an uncompromising Victorian lady. But her deeds were the epitome of charity and kindness and would benefit Savannahians for over a century.

Teflair was born into a prestigious and wealthy colonial family. Her father, Edward Telfair, became a member of the Sons of Liberty during the American Revolution, was governor of Georgia three times, and was a successful businessman.

The Telfair House, built in 1820, on Telfair Square. When Mary Telfair died in 1876, she left the house to the Georgia Historical Society. It was enlarged and opened as the Telfair Academy of Arts and Sciences in 1886. (Photo by Karri Cormican)

George Washington, on his trip through the southern colonies in 1791, spent a night at the Telfair home in Savannah. Mary, still a small child, remembered Washington's visit. But her exact age during the president's visit remains unknown. Later in life, she often changed her birth date. After she died, her passport was found and it was evident that she had tampered with her date of birth.

Though she never held public office, Mary's influence with her family and in the community grew. She was known for her religious fervor and sternness, and if she disapproved of a family member's behavior it usually meant ostracism.

THE INHERITANCE

After her father's death in 1807, the Telfair fortune was willed to Mary's older brother, Alexander. When Alexander died, the estate was bequeathed to Mary and her sister Margaret. Margaret married, but Mary would remain single all of her life.

Only three days before her death on June 2, 1875, Mary wrote her will. The bulk of her estate, close to $750,000, was earmarked for Savannah and philanthropic purposes. Outraged by the outcome of the will, relatives tried for years to contest it, but to no avail. Mary's wishes were carried out.

Mary bequeathed land to the Widow's Society and the Union Society. She left a large sum for the establishment of a woman's hospital (Telfair Hospital), and bequeathed the family mansion to the city for an arts and sciences academy, the Telfair Museum.

Mary, a life-long Presbyterian and member of the Independent Presbyterian Church, designated money for the church as well as property on the southwest corner of Bull and Broughton streets. She donated most of the Telfair family papers to the Georgia Historical Society.

Yet, with each measure of generosity, with each donation, came stipulations and conditions. It was as if Mary, though dead, still dictated, still had her way.

The terms in her will stated that if her conditions were not met then money would be withheld. The congregation at the Independent Presbyterian Church had, for years, been in a dispute over the height of the pulpit in the sanctuary. Some wanted it to remain, towering over the congregation, while others wanted it lowered. Mary favored the pulpit at the high level.

Consequently, her will states that "no material alterations or changes will be made in the pulpit or gallies of the present church." Today, the pulpit in the church remains high above the congregation.

Mary completed the building of Hodgson Hall, named for her brother-in-law, William Hodgson, to be used as a library by the Georgia Historical Society. Again, the aid was conditional. Telfair's stipulations for use of the building were clear and remain to this day. A marble tablet rests over the entrance of the building's main lobby. It reads:

> FIRST: This building is to be used exclusively for purposes connected with the business of the historical society. SECOND: No public speaking is to be permitted except addresses and lectures delivered before the historical society. THIRD: No feasting, drinking, smoking, or amusements of any kind will be permitted within its walls. FOURTH: It is not to be loaned nor rented for any purpose.

Telfair Hospital was the only institution for which Mary's stipulations were not excessive and threats of revocation were not made. Her will merely asks that a hospital for women be established and that there be "no unnecessary display connected with it."

The bequest of the Telfair mansion also came with several provisos, one of which prohibited the serving of alcoholic beverages on the premises. This request was honored for years, until guests at an art reception were served champagne. As the champagne was poured, a portion of the roof collapsed.

Did Mary Telfair, known for her stern religious principles and stubbornness, have her way once again?

She is buried at Bonaventure Cemetery next to her brother-in-law, William, and her sister, Margaret.

Andrew Bryan:
Up from Slavery

During the years of American slavery, black churches were not merely buildings made of earth and wood, but often became the bedrock of the black community. They combined a mixture of African culture and Western civilization that would develop into a unique form.

It was said during this period that conversion of a slave to Christianity freed him from the bonds of sin but not from the bonds of slavery. In this respect, it was safe for slave owners to allow a measure of religious freedom because they would not suffer economic loss. Yet, freedoms were hard to come by and even religion was infected by the intolerance of the times.

Initially, black converts were allowed to join white churches, but the situation soon became problematic. Though there were exceptions, converted blacks were usually ostracized in white churches and forced to start their own congregations. From this backdrop and period in history sprang forth many churches that still exist. Such is the case of the First Bryan Baptist Church in Savannah, the oldest black congregation in North America.

The First Bryan Baptist Church was founded in 1778, in large part due to the preaching of two black ministers—George Leile and Andrew Bryan—and two white preachers—Thomas Burton and Abraham Marshall. But it was Andrew Bryan whose dedication and service guided the congregation through its early years, laying a foundation that survives to the present.

Andrew Bryan was born into slavery around 1716 on a plantation sixteen miles south of Charleston. Not much is known of his early life, but in 1765 he was moved to Brampton Plantation, three miles from Savannah. From here he would make his mark.

According to most sources, Byran's conversion to Christianity came through the preaching of George Leile, who also began his life in slavery, gained his freedom, and finally settled in Jamaica.

EVANGELICAL AWAKENING

During the 1780s, Brampton Plantation became the center of an evangelical awakening, and slaves were converted in fields, barns, and huts. Bryan was baptized during this time and within months began to exhort fellow believers.

He and a group of forty-five slaves were granted permission by Savannahian Edward Davis to conduct services on Davis' land in Yamacraw. The small group grew steadfast in faith and devotion, but a brief and intense period of persecution began. Many whites considered any gathering of slaves as a sign of rebellion and sought to crush it.

Arrested on trumped up charges, Andrew and his brother Sampson were brought before the magistrate, beaten, and imprisoned. But Andrew Bryan's fortitude was unshakable. Charges were dropped and the brothers released.

A letter written at the time describes the scene. Andrew, who was cut and bleeding badly, told his persecutors: "I rejoice not only to be whipped, but would freely suffer death for the cause of Christ."

Things calmed after this and Bryan continued to preach. Jonathan Bryan, Andrew's master, died in 1790 and Andrew finally purchased his freedom.

FINALLY FREE

Bryan, now a free man, moved unencumbered around town and

made important connections. He purchased his first piece of property, lot number 12, North Oglethorpe ward, on June 1, 1790, for twenty-seven pounds sterling; three years later he purchased a lot on Bryan Street (now the location of First Bryan Baptist Church.)

The church continued to prosper and grow, and Bryan guided it into the beginning of the century that would see the emancipation of his people. He died on October 6, 1812, and is buried in Laurel Grove Cemetery, South.

In 1832, the congregation split into two factions. One group moved to a location on Franklin Square and formed the First African Baptist Church. The remaining faction would be known as the First Bryan Baptist Church.

This characterization of Bryan in later life, given by Dr. Henry Holcomb, a contemporary, is a fitting tribute to the man who labored, suffered, and shed his blood for racial tolerance and religious freedom:

> Andrew Bryan not only honorably obtained liberty but a handsome estate. His fleecy and well set locks have been bleached by eighty winters; and dressed like a bishop of London, he rides, moderately corpulent, in his chair, and, with manly features of jetty hue, fills any person to who he gracefully bows with pleasure and veneration, by displaying in smiles even rows of natural teeth white as ivory, and a pair of fine black eyes sparkling with intelligence, benevolence, and joy.

Johnny Mercer,
Oscar-Winning Lyricist

Johnny Mercer had an ear for music and was often found writing lyrics and singing, but he refused to take piano lessons, afraid of what the other boys might think. As a teenager he sang in the choir at St. John's Episcopal Church on Madison Square, and by age fifteen had written his first song, "Sister Suzy Struts Her Stuff," for his only sister, Juliana.

In a musical career that spanned more than four decades, Johnny Mercer penned more than 1,500 songs and won four Oscars. He worked with some of the biggest names in show business: Bing Crosby, Fred Astaire, Frank Sinatra, Nat King Cole, Ray Charles, Judy Garland, and Tony Bennett.

In 1929, at the age of nineteen, Mercer set out for New York to begin an acting career. A year passed without success, and he worked part-time as a runner on Wall Street. But his fortunes would soon change. In 1930, he persuaded a director that he could write, and Mercer's tune "Out of Breath and Scared to Death of You" was used in the Broadway revue "Garrick Gaieties." While working on this production, he met his future wife, dancer Elizabeth "Ginger" Meehan. In 1931, the soft-spoken Southerner and the Brooklyn native were married.

"Lazy Bones," Mercer's first big hit, was written in 1933. Soon, the native Savannahian, who could not read music and had never taken formal music lessons, found himself with more work than he could handle. He continued to crank out lyrics and was hired to work for the Kraft radio program. Mercer's star had risen quickly and there was only once place left to go—Hollywood.

HELLO, HOLLYWOOD

In 1935, RKO Pictures hired Mercer to write songs, sing, and act in two motion pictures, *Old Man Rhythm* and *To Beat the Band.* Though his acting career never materialized, his songwriting career continued to gain momentum. He recorded duets with Bing Crosby as well as Nat King Cole and wrote lyrics for the Benny Goodman orchestra. He appeared numerous times on "Hit Parade" and had an unprecedented number of songs remain on its charts.

During the twenty-two years "Hit Parade" was on the air, Mercer had one song on the show for 221 weeks, two for 55 weeks, and three for 6 weeks.

Mercer co-founded Capitol Records in 1942 and later became its president. By the late 1950s, his songwriting pace had slowed but he continued to produce hits.

He often appeared as a guest on many of television's early shows along with Jack Benny, Bing Crosby, and Bob Hope. He wrote his Oscar winning "The Atcheson, Topeka and the Santa Fe" in 1946, inspired by his long train rides from California to the east coast. His "In the Cool, Cool, Cool of the Evening" won an Oscar in 1952.

Yet, success did not spoil the gifted songwriter, who never forgot his roots nor the inspiration that helped him write so many of his songs. Though Mercer lived in Hollywood, he continued to keep a Savannah residence on Burnside Island. It was there that he wrote "Moon River," inspired by the river that ran behind his house.

This simple but elegant song won an Oscar in 1962. The same year the Chatham County Commission changed the name of the Back River to Moon River in Mercer's honor. Mercer won his fourth and final Oscar in 1963 for "Days of Wine and Roses."

On October 25, 1975, Mercer had to undergo surgery for a benign brain tumor. He never fully recovered and died on July 25, 1976, at his Bel Air, California, home.

His body was cremated, then interred at the Mercer family plot in Bonaventure Cemetery. In 1977, Old Tybee Road on Wilmington Island was renamed Johnny Mercer Boulevard in his honor.

The Savannah Civic Center Theater was also named in his honor. Mercer was inducted into the Georgia Music Hall of Fame in Macon in 1980. He is the only non-statesman to have a plaque hanging in the state capitol.

Archibald Bulloch,
Statesman, Patriot, Soldier

Leading a ragtag detachment of soldiers—riflemen, light infantry, volunteers, and Creek Indians—Archibald Bulloch navigated the Savannah River, crossed marsh and swamp, and landed on British-controlled Tybee Island on March 25, 1776. Surprising their enemy, the colonials torched all of the island's buildings, killed two Royal marines and one Tory, and took a marine and several Tories prisoner. All this was achieved while a

British man-of-war, anchored just off the beach, blasted the island with shot and shell.

This was just a taste of the violence that would soon follow, as America would fight seven grueling years to gain her independence. And Archibald Bulloch, three-time Georgia governor and delegate to the Continental Congress, would help lead the way.

Bulloch is credited with unifying the various factions of colonists who wanted independence, and many historians claim that without his leadership Georgia might have remained a royal colony.

Bulloch was born in Charleston around 1729, the son of a Scottish clergyman and planter. In 1750, the Bullochs relocated to Savannah and Archibald began practicing law. He married sixteen-year-year-old Mary DeVeaux on October 9, 1764; together they would have four children.

In 1768, Bulloch was elected to the Commons House, and served until 1773. He served on the committee that corresponded with Benjamin Franklin, Georgia's colonial agent in London. But when the British Parliament passed the Boston Port Bill in 1774, Bulloch became an ardent defender of liberty and one of the first Georgians to advocate independence.

The Boston Port Bill levied high taxation on Boston's goods and revoked Massachusetts's charter as a royal colony. In addition, the British, either not understanding colonial resolve or not caring, passed a bill ordering all colonists accused of crimes to be transported to England for trial.

A CALL TO ARMS

On July 20, the *Georgia Gazette* published a notice calling all Savannahians who desired liberty to attend a meeting at Tondee's Tavern. Against royal governor Wright's order, a meeting was held on July 27, 1774, and again on August 10.

The group, led by Bulloch, John Houstoun, George Walton, and Noble Jones, sympathized with the Bostonians and passed a number of resolutions. They proclaimed that the British Port Bill was an act of tyranny, that the revocation of Massachusetts's royal charter was subversive to American rights, that Parliament had no right to tax American subjects, and that Georgia concurred with her sister colonies in every constitutional measure to obtain redress for grievances.

In addition, they shipped 600 barrels of rice and a large amount of cash to Boston.

Bulloch was elected president of the Provincial Congress of Georgia on July 4, 1775. Three days later he was named a delegate to the Continental Congress in Philadelphia. In 1776, the same year he led troops against British positions on Tybee Island, Bulloch became a delegate to the Second Continental Congress. In a passionate address to his colleagues, he stated: "This is no time to talk of moderation; in the present instance it ceases to be a virtue."

Bulloch spent much of his time traveling and missed his chance to sign the Declaration of Independence. On July 7, 1776, he was elected again as president of the Provincial Congress. He was also named commander in chief of Georgia's military forces.

Unfortunately for his country, he died prematurely, on February 25, 1777. His death paved the way for the McIntosh-Gwinnett feud that would rage until the end of the war and would end in tragedy.

Bulloch left behind a twenty-nine-year-old widow and four small children. He was buried in the Colonial Cemetery in Savannah. Bulloch County was named in his honor. Years later, Eleanor Roosevelt traced her ancestry back to Bulloch. He was also President Theodore Roosevelt's great-great-grandfather.

Daniel J. Bourke:
Son of Erin, Man of Faith

In the 5th century A.D. , a young man named Patrick was taken captive from his English home and enslaved in Ireland. In this strange land, paganism and superstition flourished. Eventually gaining his freedom, Patrick returned home, but Ireland's plight burned within. He returned, not as a slave but as a missionary, and brought Christianity to a pagan Ireland.

In doing so, he became a saint. Fifteen centuries later, Saint Patrick's message and mission became embodied in Irish-born Monsignor Daniel J. Bourke.

Bourke was born in Ireland in 1909, one of two boys. Early on, he decided to enter the priesthood, but by all accounts was a sickly child and wasn't expected to live—an unlikely candidate to enter the ministry.

However, in 1934 Bourke graduated from All Hallows' Seminary in Dublin, Ireland, a seminary that exclusively trained young priests for the mission field. Bourke's classmates were soon scattered to the four corners of the earth, finding themselves in Australia, South America, Europe, and the United States.

According to Sister Mary Faith of the Savannah Diocese, who often talked with the monsignor about his life, his ministry, and his experiences, Bourke was scheduled to go to Washington State, but his destination was changed because Savannah's climate was more suited to his health.

Ironically, Bourke outlived his classmates, and he spent his adult years as a robust, healthy man known for his long walks and unforgettably firm handshake.

In 1934, only three months after graduation, Bourke stepped off the train in Georgia. The next sixty-three years would find him serving in the Diocese of Savannah.

Bourke's first appointment was as assistant pastor of Blessed Sacrament Parish. Seven years later, in 1942, he served as the church's administrator. He was rector from 1941 to 1945.

During these early years, Monsignor Bourke's charm, unique character, and faith became evident. He is described as adamantly faithful to the teachings of the church, and as one who loved people, both Catholic and non-Catholic.

"I am loyal to the Holy Father [the Pope], and down the line with the traditional church, not the dissidents," he would later write.

Between 1945 and 1970, Bourke ministered at churches in Albany and Augusta, before returning to Savannah. After his return to Savannah, he would remain there for the balance of his life.

Bourke was the first to fill the newly created position of comptroller of the diocese, 1970-1972, and later became rector of the

Cathedral of Saint John the Baptist. He was particularly proud of the cathedral, proud that the magnificent structure was built to the glory of God, proud that it was constructed by a people possessing little worldly wealth.

Fond of telling stories and with a keen interest in politics, Monsignor Bourke met with President John F. Kennedy when he visited Savannah. Until his death, a photograph of Bourke and the president was proudly displayed in the monsignor's study.

Bourke retired in 1976 but never slowed down. He continued to be a presence in both the church and the community, and his unique Irish brogue, wit, wisdom, and love of Savannah became legendary.

GRAND MARSHALL

Finally in 1997, at the age of eighty-seven, Bourke became the oldest person and just the second priest to be named grand marshall of Savannah's Saint Patrick's Day parade.

Walking the entire three miles of the parade route, the monsignor accomplished a feat not often emulated by his more youthful predecessors.

Bourke loved Saint Patrick's Day but believed that the festivities had gotten out of hand. "The parade is well constructed," he stated, "but the parade committee has no control over the hundreds of thousands of people coming to town to join the party and most of them aren't Irish. To them, Saint Patrick's Day is a pagan's good time.

On September 3, 1998, only eighteen months after Bourke's saunter as parade grand marshall, he fell in the sacristy at Blessed Sacrament Church while vesting for Mass. Within two weeks he was dead.

At Catholic Cemetery on Wheaton Street, a tearful flock of faithful followers laid Monsignor Daniel J. Bourke to rest. He still lives in the hearts and minds of those he ministered to, of those he touched.

Gordon Saussy,
Coach, Judge, Politician

During the last decade of the 19th century, college and professional football were in their infancy. Men usually played without helmets, and when helmets were used, they were little more than straps of leather. Pads were sparse and rules protecting players against injury were nonexistent.

On a frigid November day in 1893, two young Savannahians, Gordon and Hugh Saussy, found themselves playing for a semi-pro team in New York under such circumstances. But tragedy soon struck. Hugh broke his neck in a game and died.

But Gordon continued to play. The next year he enrolled at Cornell University and played football, but under an assumed name. After the death of his brother, the Saussy family disapproved of the game.

The next season young Saussy, a tailback, had the privilege of playing with future football legend Pop Warner. This association would have a profound and lasting impact on Saussy's life.

Graduating from Cornell with a law degree in 1896, Saussy returned to Savannah and helped form the city's first semi-pro team. In 1897, Warner became head coach at the University of Georgia and persuaded Saussy to become an assistant. The next season, Warner left for another coaching job and in 1899, Saussy, at age twenty-five, became the youngest head coach in the University of Georgia's history. He is also the only Savannahian ever to hold the job.

Though Saussy's team compiled a 2-3-1 record, the wins included beating Clemson in the first game of the season, 11-0, and defeating the hated Georgia Tech Yellow Jackets in Athens by a score of 33-0. Georgia's only tie of the season, against Auburn, was a controversial one. Auburn led by an 11-6 score with a minute left on the clock when an unruly mob prevented the official conclusion of the game. The game was declared a tie and the record books recorded a 0-0 score.

Saussy returned to Savannah in 1900 and practiced law, reared a family, and in time threw his hat into the political arena.

He traveled to New York to study the New York Port Authority's operations. Returning to Georgia, he spent most of 1924 in Atlanta working with the state legislature trying to pass a bill for the creation of the Savannah Port Authority. The next year, he authored the piece of legislation that brought the port authority to life.

Saussy became Savannah's 109th mayor on January 29, 1929, in an unopposed election. He was reelected for a second term but resigned within four months to run for the position of probate judge vacated by the death of Judge Henry McAlpin. Saussy won the election and held the position until his death twenty-one years later.

Saussy was an avid sportsman who loved to hunt quail and keep abreast of the Georgia Bulldogs. He was on hand in 1929 to watch the University play Yale to dedicate Sanford Stadium.

Grandson Gordon Saussy Varnedoe remembers his grandfather as a larger-than-life figure. Following in his footsteps, Varnedoe, who graduated from Georgia, played for the Bulldogs during spring practice in 1960. He made it through the spring and as a backup fullback received handoffs from future National Football League hall-of-famer Fran Tarkenton.

Saussy died in 1952 after a life devoted to the law. He is remembered as an athlete, coach, fierce competitor, politician, lawyer, judge, and devoted family man.

Edward C. Anderson:
Mayor Becomes Arms Dealer

Anderson walked down a dimly lit street in London. The English fog began to close in and he turned his collar against the cold. Turning a corner, he glanced behind and noticed two men following him. He reached in his coat for the reassurance of his revolver, hoping he would not have to use it. Mustering his courage, he turned to face the two men. Surprised, they quickly fled.

Breathing a sigh of relief, he entered a tavern and ordered a Scotch. As soon as he took a swallow he realized that he'd been drugged, but the effect of one glass wasn't enough to render him unconscious. Once more, he had thwarted the stratagems of his adversaries.

This isn't a scene from a mystery. It's just one of the many exploits of native Savannahian Edward C. Anderson.

Anderson, former U.S. naval officer, Savannah mayor (1855-1857), planter, and businessman, had recently cast his lot with the newly formed Confederacy, though at great personal distress.

He wrote:

> I disapproved entirely of the rash course of the politicians of the country North and South and believed that Georgia had been led by the nose by South Carolina. I had been reared under the US flag in the Navy and was to the innermost recess of my nature, attached to its fold, yet the die was cast & my lot as a Southern man with it.

The year 1861 found Confederate President Jefferson Davis in a bind. Facing the might of the Federal army, he had few munitions and sparse resources. In response, he summoned Anderson to the Confederate capital and dispatched him on a secret mission to purchase war materials.

Anderson sailed for England on May 25, 1861. The timing of his mission was crucial; he had to act quickly before the tightening Federal blockade completely sealed Southern ports.

On the afternoon of June 21, 1861, Anderson arrived in England and began negotiations for war materials. Immediately identified, he was stalked by American agents and hired British detectives. They thwarted Anderson's first attempt to purchase arms.

On July 29, 1861, a frustrated Anderson wrote:

> Secured 17,000 muskets from Graysbrook. After the bargain had been made and the guns ordered to be prepared for shipment, the guns were sold to a Yankee contractor and he attempted to excuse it by stating that the sale had been made by his subordinate without his knowledge or approval.

On several occasions Anderson would secure an order for munitions only to have a U.S. agent block the transaction with British customs. Often Anderson was simply outbid by American agents who had more cash and extensive credit, while he often traded in cotton.

Despite these difficulties, Anderson's accomplishments in England were remarkable. Numerous times he spotted spies and turned the tables on them by supplying them with false information. His insight into human nature and solid business sense kept him one step ahead of his foes, and he managed to secure a number of shipments of muskets from different foundries and sent them across the Atlantic to Dixie.

One of Anderson's boldest feats was the supplying of the *Bermuda,* an 898-ton, 216-foot brig. With a cargo of guns and supplies valued at $250,000, the *Bermuda* ran the Union blockade and arrived safely in Savannah on September 17, 1861.

Encouraged by this success, Anderson worked fervently. He was instrumental in the building of the *Oreto,* a twin-bladed steamer, built under guise as a British merchant ship.

The *Oreto* set sail on March 22, 1862. As soon as she reached international waters, the Union Jack was lowered, the Confederate colors raised, a new crew added, and the ship commissioned the *CSS Florida.*

The *Florida,* a cruiser and commerce raider, played havoc with Northern merchant ships, ushering in a reign of terror. Operating under international law, the Southern raider captured Union ships, removed their crews, and set the vessels ablaze. Later, several of the captured ships were commissioned into the Confederate Navy.

The *Florida* and her sister ship, the *CSS Alabama,* were called the scourge of the seas and all but shut down Northern shipping for two years.

Yet, Anderson's greatest achievement in Britain was the purchase and supplying of the *Fingal.* The *Fingal,* displacing 800 tons, was personally escorted away from the English coast by Anderson. Like the *Florida,* the *Fingal* was commissioned into Confederate service as soon as the English shore faded over the horizon. She would later be converted into the ironclad *CSS Atlanta* and patrol the waterways and inlets around Savannah.

An impressive array of war materiel was on board the *Fingal:* 15,000 Enfield rifles (a few of the rifles are on display at Fort Jackson); 1,000,000 cartridges; 2,000,000 percussion caps; 3,000 cavalry sabers; 500 revolvers; two, 2½-inch cannons and two, 24½-inch rifled cannons, along with 8,000 shells (one of the cannons is mounted atop the parapets on Fort Pulaski); 400 barrels of gunpowder, and large quantities of blankets, medicine, and clothing.

Setting sail for the Azores Islands, 800 miles south of Portugal, the *Fingal* arrived on October 23, 1862, to replenish her water supply. U.S. agents waited as the ship made port and tried to have authorities impound her, but to no avail. She crossed the Atlantic without further interruption, ran the blockade off the Georgia coast, and received a hero's welcome in Savannah. This was the pinnacle of Anderson's war career but from there it would be downhill.

Anderson received new orders and was appointed to oversee construction of Georgia's coastal batteries. Upon his shoulders lay the responsibility of installing armaments at Fort Jackson, Skidaway, and Thunderbolt batteries, and batteries at White Bluff and Isle of Hope, Fort McAllister, Hutchinson Island, and Wilmington Island. But Anderson despised his new assignment and disliked the officers he commanded, believing them to be lacking in intelligence and ill-prepared for war.

He pleaded with Robert E. Lee, commander of Georgia's coastal defenses during the first year of the war, for a different assignment but without success. Anderson would remain in Savannah for the balance of the war, longing to return to Europe as an agent or to see action in the field.

On the night of December 20, 1864, as Sherman's 60,000 troops prepared to envelope Savannah, Anderson, along with 10,000 Confederates commanded by Gen. William Hardee, slipped across the Savannah River on pontoon bridges.

Savannah surrendered and on December 21, 1864, after an absence of nearly four years, the American flag snapped in the Savannah breeze.

As the once-proud and defiant Confederacy crumbled around him, Anderson arrived in Charleston to help the city beef up its defenses. He would remain in South Carolina until the surrender less than four months away.

After the war, Anderson returned to Savannah, and on December 6, 1865, became the city's first postwar mayor in the first voting allowed after the city's capitulation. He worked tire-lessly to improve the city's infrastructure and served as mayor until October 18, 1869.

After Anderson left office he turned to private business endeav-ors, but continued to be active in civic affairs. He lobbied in Washington for his native city and secured an audience with President Grant and General Sherman, both of whom showed interest in improving conditions in Savannah.

Persuaded to run again for mayor, Anderson won his fourth and final term in 1873. In his last term he negotiated a contract with the Federal government to dredge the Savannah River and contin-ued to work on Savannah's economic development.

After Anderson left office, he led an active life in business, civic, and religious affairs. He died on January 6, 1883. The *Savannah News* printed an extensive obituary listing Anderson's accomplishments as a U.S. naval officer, Confederate officer, mayor, and community leader.

On a cold winter day in January, he was laid to rest in Laurel Grove Cemetery. The man, once torn between loyalty to country and loyalty to state, was mourned by fellow Savannahians, fellow Georgians, former comrades, and former adversaries.

John Wesley, Founder of Methodism

In a life spanning nearly nine decades, John Wesley influenced millions. Yet before he was known as the founder of Methodism he spent time in Savannah. And it was in Savannah that the young clergyman fell in love, was brought before a jury on defamation charges, and fled the city in a cloud of suspicion.

Wesley was born in Epsworth, England, on June 17, 1703, the fifteenth of nineteen children. At age seventeen he enrolled in Christ College at Oxford.

The John Wesley monument in Reynolds Square, near the site of his 1735 parish house. (Photo courtesy Henderson Studios, Savannah)

TO PROSELYTIZE THE COLONIES

Wesley finished his studies at Christ College, and on September 19, 1725, received his ordination in the Anglican Church. In 1729, Wesley went into residence at Oxford as a fellow of Lincoln College. There he formed a group called the Holy Club, a group of students, including his brother Charles and George Whitefield, who adhered to a strict moral code. Soon they were called Methodists—a term of derision—because of their methodical religious practices.

Wesley developed a keen interest in the British colonies and in 1735 arrived in Georgia to build his parish. Having lofty goals, he planned to proselytize the Indians and convert as many Savannahians as possible. Unfortunately, his stern and regimented ways became a point of contention.

The young clergyman became one of the most unpopular men in town, and on one occasion was even threatened at gunpoint by one of his offended female parishioners.

Unsuccessful in his religious endeavors, Wesley accepted a position as Gen. James Oglethorpe's secretary. While working for Oglethorpe, Wesley met Savannah's chief magistrate Thomas Causton.

LOVE GONE BAD

Through Causton he met native Savannahian Sophia Hopkey, Causton's niece.

Sophia, only eighteen when she met Wesley, is described as tall and slender with hazel eyes and light brown hair. Wesley, on the other hand, was thirty-three years old, only 5-feet, 4-inches tall, and described as having undistinguished features.

Within a few months Sophia began to take French lessons from Wesley, and when he fell ill she nursed him back to health. Consequently, a short, intense, but controversial love affair developed.

But when the subject of marriage came up, Wesley, torn between his love for Sophia and the ministry, floundered. Though not prohibited from marrying by the Anglican Church, Wesley believed that a minister should not marry, fearing that his love for Sophia would outgrow his love for God.

Frustrated with Wesley's indecision, Sophia discontinued her French lessons and sought help from her uncle.

Causton made it clear. He told Wesley: "I give her to you. Do what you will with her. Take her into your own hand. Promise her what you will. I will make it good." Several months elapsed but a tormented, struggling Wesley still could not commit.

Finally, in March 1736, Causton contacted Wesley and requested that he announce the intended marriage of Sophia and her new fiancé, Mr. William Williamson. Wesley refused. Sophia and Williamson eloped as a result, violating church ordinances on marriage.

After her marriage to Williamson, Sophia neglected church attendance and habitually missed communion.

Wesley, frustrated and hurt, charged her with hypocrisy and neglect of public church services. When she did return to church, however, Wesley refused to allow her to participate in communion services. Causton, outraged, issued a warrant charging Wesley with defamation, and set a court hearing for August 22.

HAULED INTO COURT

Before a group of supporters, Causton presented a list of grievances explaining why Wesley was unfit to continue as minister. The situation intensified when Wesley was found guilty on some, but not all, of the counts. Several infractions were deemed ecclesiastical in nature and outside the court's jurisdiction. Instead of facing charges, Wesley fled to Charleston. Within a few days he secured passage for a return trip to England.

Though he left in disgrace, his days in Georgia were not wasted. He credited his Savannah stay as a time of maturation and soul searching. Fifteen years later, at the age of forty-eight, Wesley finally married, but the marriage was unsuccessful and within a year he and his wife were living apart. In a few months, she died. He never remarried.

By the time Wesley died in 1791 at the age of eighty-eight, his contribution to Protestantism, Christianity, and Western Civilization was enormous. He wrote over 400 books, including biographies, devotionals, English, French, Latin, Hebrew, and Greek grammars, and treatises on logic, medicine, literary criticism, theology, history, and philosophy. Many of his books were sold cheaply so the poor could afford them.

In England, he rallied in support of labor laws to protect workers and was an advocate for the poor and suffering. It has been estimated that he traveled over 250,000 miles on horseback preaching the gospel. And from his life's work, Methodism, one of the largest Protestant churches in the world, has flourished.

But for all of his accomplishments and fame, Wesley never forgot Sophia. Even in his later years, he often wrote about her and his Savannah sojourn in his private journal.

Gen. Frank O'Driscoll Hunter:
On a Wing and a Prayer

Before the field of aviation gained respect, before it became practical, Savannahian Frank Hunter gleaned from it all he could. In return, he gained a career, became a legend, and lived a life many only dream of.

Frank O' Driscoll Hunter was born on December 8, 1894. As a small boy he earned the nickname "Monk" for his unsaintly behavior, a name that would remain with him for the rest of his life. As a teenager he attended the prestigious Hotchkiss Preparatory School in Connecticut. Though he did not excel in his studies, his mischievous behavior earned him the attention of the school's administration. He was known for his athletic ability, spunk, sharp clothes, good looks, and poor relations with the faculty.

After finishing school, Hunter headed to New York and became a securities salesman, a job that he loathed. By this time, World War I had broken out and Hunter kept abreast of its development. He longed to have the chance to fly and on May 18, 1917, joined the U.S. Army, aviation section, as a sergeant. On September 12, 1917, he began flight training as a newly commissioned first lieutenant.

After only four and a half hours of dual instruction Hunter flew solo, and after only nine hours graduated from flight school.

Gen. Frank O'Driscoll Hunter (center) with friend and flying ace Eddie Rickenbacker (left). (Photo courtesy U.S. Army, Fort Stewart, Georgia)

Within a few days Hunter boarded the steamer *St. Louis* bound for Liverpool and on October 22 arrived in England. He was assigned to the 103rd Aero Squadron based in France and would soon taste battle.

FIRST TASTE OF WAR

Eager to prove himself, Hunter challenged two German fighters on his first mission. The results were less than glorious. His plane suffered a broken windshield and a ruptured fuel tank (which showered Hunter with aviation fuel), was pierced by several bullets, had four inches shot off the propeller, and had a right strut damaged. Bleeding badly from a wound in the forehead, Hunter struggled to return to the airfield in France. But he would not give up, and within days was in the air again engaging the enemy.

AMERICAN ACE

In May 1918, Hunter joined the famous 94th Squadron, commanded by Eddie Rickenbacker, and within a few months had downed five enemy planes, earning the much-coveted title of ace. By war's end he added three additional victories for a total of eight confirmed kills.

He was one of only sixty American aces and Georgia's only flying ace during the war. For his services he won five Distinguished Flying Crosses with four Oak Leaf Clusters, a Purple Heart, a French Croix d 'Guerre, and five citations for heroism.

Armistice was signed on November 11, 1919, and by February Hunter was discharged from the service. He returned to Savannah, but civilian life did not agree with the spirited pilot. In less than two years he reenlisted and again received an officer's commission.

Between the world wars Hunter became an army test pilot and flew virtually every type and modification of fighter developed, becoming instrumental in helping the army's aviation program to maturity.

In 1923, while participating in a flying circus for charity, Hunter flew into heavy fog, crashed-landed in a field, and suffered a broken back. Recuperation took nearly a year, but he returned to the cockpit. In fact, on several occasions Hunter saved his life by parachuting, thus becoming a member of the Caterpillar Club, those flyers who have parachuted to safety.

He crashed again in 1933 in an experimental plane and broke his back a second time; again recuperation took close to a year and again he returned to flying.

By 1940, Hunter was one of only six flying aces left in the army. The same year, Hunter Army Airfield in Savannah was named in his honor, making him the first living person to have a military base named after him.

During World War II, Hunter commanded fighter squadrons that launched offensive sweeps against Nazi positions in France and rose in rank from colonel to brigadier general to major general. By the end of the war he had added additional hardware to his war chest by winning the Distinguished Service Medal and the Legion of Merit.

Hunter retired from the military in 1947 and returned to

Savannah, where he was active in civic affairs. Later in life he listed cocktail parties, women, and fishing as his favorite hobbies. He died on June 25, 1982. He was buried at Laurel Grove Cemetery with full military honors.

Dr. Richard Arnold, Caring Physician and Mayor

Physician, politician, and businessman, Richard Arnold lived a life equal in achievements to that of two men. His concern for the sick and his commitment to disease prevention were the hallmarks of his medical career. His politics were mixed with both diplomacy and fierce Southern loyalty.

Arnold was born in 1808. By age ten he had suffered the death of his mother. One of her last requests was that her children be educated in the "Northern States." Arnold would spend the balance of his youth away from home.

Arnold graduated from Princeton in 1926 and from the University of Pennsylvania School of Medicine in 1832. After a brief trip to Europe, he returned to Savannah, began his medical career, and acquired half ownership of the *Guardian,* serving as the newspaper's editor until 1835.

On September 12, 1842, Arnold was appointed mayor by a board of aldermen. He was the last mayor to hold the office without being elected. On December 12 of the same year, the state legislature authorized mayoral elections.

His first term expired on September 11, 1843, and he concentrated on his medical practice and raising a family, but tragedy would soon strike. In 1850, Richard suffered the death of his wife. Many close to him said that he never recovered from her loss and that grief plagued him for the rest of his life.

The next year, on December 8, 1851, Arnold began his second mayoral term, this time being elected, and served until December 9, 1852.

Seven years elapsed before he sought a third term as mayor. During these years he was active in the Medical Association of Georgia and helped the American Medical Association, becoming its first secretary as well as serving in the state legislature.

He worked tirelessly during the yellow fever epidemic of 1854, but was frustrated with the inadequate knowledge offered by the medical community. A newspaper during this time stated, "For six consecutive weeks Dr. Arnold, attending the sick and dying, averaged only four hours of sleep daily."

As a result of witnessing so many deaths, this physician became a medical pioneer in seeking causes for what were then called the "baffling diseases." He received wide acclaim, north and south, for his studies on tropical fevers.

On October 17, 1859, Arnold was elected to a third term as mayor. During this term he reorganized the police department, adding several new officers and staff members.

His third term expired on October 15, 1860, and he turned his political energies to the approaching clouds of war between North and South. Despite his close ties to the North, he became a delegate to the state constitutional convention on secession and supported ratification of an ordinance of secession.

Yet, his ardent Southern loyalty had an ironic twist. It was Dr. Arnold and a delegation of alderman who walked down Bay Street to meet the first Union troops entering the city. He was severely criticized at the time for complying with Union authority, but necessity often dictates politics. Confederate troops in Savannah had recently evacuated, leaving the city defenseless. He finished his fourth and last mayoral term on December 11, 1865.

After the war, Arnold served as president of the school board until his death, at age sixty-seven, in July 1876. The prominent physician, medical researcher, politician, and longtime mayor was finally laid to rest in Bonaventure Cemetery. Years later, Arnold Street and Richard Arnold High School were named in his honor.

— ∞ —

Gen. Lachlan McIntosh,
Valiant Scot, Controversial Patriot

The smoke from their black powder pistols had not yet cleared the air when two of America's founders lay in a pool of blood. Lachlan McIntosh would live and continue to serve his country; Button Gwinnett would die an untimely death. Both men came to symbolize the 18th century method of defending one's honor—the duel.

Born in Scotland in 1727, Lachlan McIntosh was the son of John McIntosh, of the Borlam branch of the Clan McIntosh. His family fell from prominence during the Scottish Rebellion of 1715. Eventually having their land confiscated, they fled to the American colonies in 1736 with Gen. James Oglethorpe on his second trip to Georgia. On board were over 130 Highlanders.

After arriving in Savannah, the McIntosh family settled on the banks of the Altamaha River, near the site of present-day Darien. Ever ready to wield the sword, John McIntosh joined Oglethorpe's offensive into Spanish-controlled Florida in 1734, but was captured around St. Augustine and imprisoned. Soon he was on his way to Spain, where he would spend several years in a Spanish cell. On November 13, Lachlan and his brother were taken under Oglethorpe's wing and placed in his brigade as cadets where they received a rudimentary education in arithmetic and English.

Four years elapsed and Lachlan moved to Charleston to work in the mercantile trade for Henry Laurens, the first American minister to Holland and the pre-Revolutionary War president of the Georgia Congress. In Charleston, Lachlan completed his studies. He was described at the time as "exibiting [sic] a fine, manly appearance, and passion, and a calm, fine temper." No mean feat for a young Scotchman raised at the knee of Scottish warriors.

BACK TO GEORGIA

Lachlan returned to the family plantation in Georgia, married, and became a land surveyor. As such, he accumulated massive tracts of land and subsequent wealth. He spent the next two decades in relative quiet.

During the mid-1770s, McIntosh joined the debate against the British Crown and ardently supported the independence movement. In January 1775, he led a committee in Darien that denounced violations of colonial rights and called for support of Georgia's Provincial Congress and the First Continental Congress in Philadelphia. By July 4 of that year McIntosh sat as a delegate of the Georgia Provincial Congress. Six months later he received a colonel's commission.

In March 1776, McIntosh led 300 troops in the first overt act of war in Georgia. When British troops tried to seize cargoes of rice on ships in the Savannah River, McIntosh mounted three cannon atop of Yamacraw Bluff and shelled the British. By day's end, the British withdrew. This action was later referred to as the "Battle of Rice Boats."

In September, an additional three regiments were placed in McIntosh's command and he was promoted to brigadier general. A few months later, he led a series of raids against the Spanish in Florida. This would serve as the background for the political activities igniting the controversy with Button Gwinnett.

GWINNETT—McINTOSH CONTROVERSY

When Archibald Bulloch died prematurely in February 1777, Button Gwinnett succeeded Bulloch as president of the Provincial Congress. Jealous of McIntosh's success, Gwinnett ordered another Florida invasion. But this time, Gwinnett—with little or no military training—bypassed McIntosh's authority and led troops on an ill-fated expedition.

Though humiliated and furious, McIntosh held his peace, at least for a time. But when Gwinnett left office, McIntosh leveled serious accusations against his character, calling him a scoundrel. Insulted, Gwinnett demanded justice and a duel between the two was set.

On the morning of May 15, 1777, at four paces—about 12 feet apart—pistols were fired. Both men were hit. McIntosh recovered. Four days later, Gwinnett died.

Public outcry against McIntosh ran high, resulting in a trial. Though acquitted, his reputation was irrevocably damaged. He appealed to Gen. George Washington for a transfer and joined the Continental Army in Pennsylvania.

McIntosh returned to Savannah in time to participate in the city's defense. He also fought in the siege of Charleston and was taken prisoner by the British when the city fell. After the war, he made his home at 110 E. Oglethorpe Street. He died in 1806 at the age of seventy-nine.

Few men have served their country so well, even though he did kill one of the country's founders.

John Deveaux, Voice of Moderation

At a time when black Americans enjoyed few freedoms and little opportunity, one carved a niche for himself. In doing so, he contributed not only to the black community but to his city, state, and nation.

John Deveaux was born in Savannah in 1848 as a free person of color. Not much is known about his childhood, but his literacy, writings, career as newspaper editor, and government service indicate that he received a formal education.

If so, his education would have occurred at the black school illegally operated by Mary Woodhouse. Before the end of slavery, "Black Codes" were enforced, making it an illegal act to teach black children how to read and write.

A TASTE OF WAR

When the Civil War erupted, Deveaux was only thirteen years of age and an unlikely candidate to see service for the fledgling Confederacy. But at age sixteen, in 1864, Deveaux served as an officer's steward aboard the Confederate ironclad *Georgia*. The *Georgia* patrolled the numerous waterways and inlets of coastal Georgia, often steaming up the Savannah River and stopping just short of cannon range of Union-controlled Fort Pulaski. Deveaux's service aboard the vessel, however, would have an ironic twist toward the end of his life.

After the war Deveaux became interested in politics and in 1870, at the age of twenty-two, received a job as clerk in the United States Customs Service. (He would serve the next thirty-nine years in the Customs Service.)

Two years later, in 1872, Deveaux turned to domestic matters and married Fannie Moore; together they had five children.

Deveaux began his career as a newspaperman in 1875, becoming editor and business manager of the *Savannah Tribune*. As editor Deveaux was dedicated to helping the cause of black citizens, encouraging their community involvement, and seeking equal justice.

Interested in military service, Deveaux was commissioned as a major of the First Battalion, Georgia State Troops, Colored Local Militia, U.S. Army in 1881. He eventually advanced to the rank of lieutenant colonel and in 1899, when the Spanish-American War erupted, became commander of all black troops in the state of Georgia.

Wanting to taste combat, Deveaux offered the services of his men to the governor and the president, but both declined. Yet, in 1901, the Georgia General Assembly honored him with the rank of lieutenant colonel for life.

Though counter to popular sentiment, Deveaux in 1889 was appointed collector of customs at the port of Brunswick, Georgia. His hard work and service eventually earned the respect of both the white and black community, and he was praised for remaining at his post and rendering service to those in need during the yellow fever epidemic of 1892-1893.

In 1897, President William McKinley appointed Deveaux as collector of customs for the port of Savannah. Again the native Savannahian faced heavy opposition, but the black community rallied in support of his appointment and he served with distinction.

Over three decades after the end of the Civil War a young worker at Laurel Grove Cemetery noticed a distinguished-looking black man laying a memorial wreath at the grave of a Confederate sailor.

He wondered: What connection did this man have with a long-forgotten fallen Confederate serviceman? When asked, Deveaux replied: "I was an enlisted man in the Confederate States Navy and had the honor of serving under the brave man buried here. I was with Lieutenant Pelot the night he was killed boarding the blockading Union warship Water Witch."

In 1909, at the age of sixty-one, Deveaux, a voice of reason and moderation and pursuer of justice, died. Many in the white community viewed Deveaux as little more than a black Republican politician riding the crest of Reconstruction. But there were those who rose above the mores of the time and appreciated the man, his contributions, his work, and above all his character. He was buried in Laurel Grove Cemetery, South, and eulogized in the *Savannah Tribune* as a man "void of selfishness, who rarely spoke ill of anyone, and a friend to many."

Eugenia Price, Unlikely Southern Novelist

While growing up in West Virginia, Eugenia Price heard teachers proclaim that West Virginia did not secede during the Civil War, and therefore was not a Southern state. Instead, it was a Mid-Atlantic state. This made an enormous impact on Price. Until she visited Georgia decades later, Eugenia made every effort to avoid the South.

She wrote: "Until moving to Georgia I hated everything about the South and never traveled further south than Virginia." Ironically, it was the South and its history that Eugenia spent thirty-five years writing about.

The daughter of a dentist, Eugenia was born in Charleston, West Virginia, on June 22, 1916. At the age of sixteen she enrolled at Ohio University. Soon she followed in her father's footsteps, completing three years of study at Northwestern Dental School in Chicago. But Eugenia left just before the start of her senior year to devote herself to writing.

It didn't take long for Eugenia to secure employment, however.

By 1939, she was writing scripts for soap operas, first in Chicago, then in New York, and finally in Cincinnati, the corporate headquarters of Proctor & Gamble. Yet, an unexpected event in Eugenia's life unfolded, taking her writing career in a different direction.

In the late 1940s Eugenia had what many called "an intense conversion to Christianity." She left her soap-writing job and turned to writing inspirational books. During the next ten years Eugenia authored two dozen religious books and received national recognition.

IN THE DEEP SOUTH

In 1961, Eugenia and longtime friend, fellow writer, and traveling companion Joyce Blackburn traveled to Florida for a bookseller's convention. On their way they decided to stop for a short trip at St. Simon's Island. Eugenia was immediately intrigued. While wandering through an old cemetery she happened upon the grave of Anson Dodge and his wives, Ellen and Anna. She decided to research their history and came up with an idea for a novel, *Beloved Invader.* Within two years Eugenia would build a house on the island and become a permanent resident.

Beloved Invader, a combination of history and biography, tells the story of a brokenhearted Episcopal priest, the Rev. Anson Dodge, who came to St. Simons after the end of the Civil War. It was the first in a series of historical quartets and trilogies that would help bring worldwide attention to coastal Georgia.

Her next two books, *Lighthouse* and *New Moon Rising,* would complete her St. Simons trilogy. Next, she turned her attention to Savannah.

BEFORE *MIDNIGHT IN THE GARDEN*

Before *Midnight in the Garden of Good and Evil,* Eugenia's Savannah novels brought thousands to the area intent on visiting the places mentioned in her books. Conducting much of her research at the Georgia Historical Society on Whitaker Street, she was a painstakingly accurate and thorough researcher.

And her diligence showed. Her Savannah quartet—*Savannah,*

To See Your Face Again, Before Darkness Falls, and *Stranger in Savannah*—was immediately popular with readers and sold millions of copies.

Eugenia's 19th century Savannah included duels fought over minor offenses, robber barons, criminals who thieved and murdered along the wharves, and villains whose codes of honor are horribly twisted to serve their own ends.

Despite Eugenia's popularity and success, literary critics didn't take her writing seriously. This bothered Eugenia and is evident in her book *Inside One Author's Heart.*

"Down their noses," she wrote in it. "I am considered by some critics a writer of merely popular books."

Yet, the facts of her success are indisputable. By the time of her death in 1996, she had authored thirty-nine books and sold twenty million copies, and her works had been printed in eighteen different languages.

Ironically, Eugenia struggled greatly with the very issues she wrote about. She admitted to not being a Southerner and later in her life confessed to "lifelong prejudices held against white southerners" since her childhood days in West Virginia. She finally came to terms with this issue in the last book of her Savannah quartet, *Stranger in Savannah.* The novel is a love story set against the politics of slavery as the country is headed toward a long and bloody civil war. In it, Eugenia's anti-slavery views are evident.

"Slavery was a way of life, the backbone of the southern economy," Price wrote. "But there were so many southerners who saw that it would defeat their economy eventually."

Her last novel, *The Waiting Time,* set in pre-Civil War Darien, Georgia, was completed just a week before her death on May 28, 1996.

Eugenia was buried in the cemetery at Christ Church on St. Simons Island, the very place where she had stumbled across the grave of Anson Dodge, fallen in love with the island, and begun the first page of a new American literary genre.

Robert Anderson,
General and Police Chief

When hostilities erupted between North and South in 1861, native Savannahian Robert Anderson, like many other Southern men, was torn between loyalty to state and loyalty to country.

Judged harshly by modern standards, the choice these men faced was trying. In the mid-19th century, a person's state was often considered his homeland, and to her he owed his first allegiance. Not to hold that allegiance was often considered treasonous. Only after the end of the Civil War did the concept fully develop of a nation, a unified whole.

Against this backdrop, young Anderson heard the troubling news that Georgia had seceded from the Union. From Fort Walla Walla, Washington, the 1857 West Point graduate resigned his commission in the U.S. Army, returned to Savannah, and received a lieutenant's commission in the Confederate army and an assignment as a staff officer.

In July 1862, he was promoted to major of the 1st Battalion Georgia Sharpshooters.

FIGHTING YANKEE IRONCLADS

The year 1862 found Yankee ironclads steaming up the Ogeechee River and cannonading Fort McAllister. Anderson commanded the troops that successfully defended the fort. McAllister remained in Confederate hands until Sherman's destructive thrust through Georgia two summers later.

In January 1863, Anderson received a colonel's commission and command of the 5th Georgia Volunteer Cavalry. The 5th Georgia Cavalry reached a force of nearly 1,000 men during its heyday and was made up of men from coastal Georgia, including Chatham, Liberty, Bulloch, Screven, McIntosh, Tattnall, and Effingham counties.

The 5th Georgia first made camp at Isle of Hope, seven miles south of Savannah. While the war in the east intensified, the 5th

Bust of Gen. Robert H. Anderson in Bonaventure Cemetery.
(Photo by the author)

Georgia remained in the backwaters, patrolling the coasts of Georgia, northern Florida, and lower South Carolina, seeing limited action, often skirmishing with Union gunboats and engaging small squads of Federal infantry.

Small detachments of the 5th Georgia did, however, participate in the Battle of Olustee, the only campaign waged, although unsuccessfully, to bring Florida back into the Union.

OFF TO FIGHT MR. SHERMAN

Shortly after the battle of Olustee, Anderson and his Confederate horsemen again took up the task of patrolling the Georgia coast. But Anderson was growing impatient and wanted to be in the thick of battle in either North Georgia or Virginia. On May 21, 1864, he wrote a heartfelt letter to Richmond asking for either a transfer to active service or to be relieved of his command.

But as the fortunes of war would dictate, the order had already been given for Anderson and the 5th Georgia to join Fightin' Joe Wheeler's Cavalry Corps, under Gen. Joseph Johnston, commander of the Army of Tennessee. It was a desperate attempt to quell the Federal juggernaut bearing down on Atlanta.

Anderson and the 5th Georgia Cavalry proceeded to Atlanta via Augusta where part of the regiment was transported by rail.

He led his unit in some of the war's fiercest fighting (the battles of the Atlanta Campaign and Sherman's March to the Sea), and the records show Anderson's exploits: cavalry raids, pistol and saber clashes, heartache, and sacrifice.

Yet, no amount of valor or sacrifice could subdue the overwhelming numbers of soldiers in blue. Less than a year after Anderson and his unit were dispatched to Atlanta, the war was over and the Confederacy lay in ruin.

During the last year of the war, Anderson was promoted to brigadier general. He later was severely wounded and in April 1865 finally surrendered.

At the close of the war, Anderson returned to Savannah and became a merchant and opened an insurance agency. In 1867, he became Savannah's police chief, serving twenty-two years until his death.

Under Anderson's leadership, the police force was reorganized and modernized, and he was instrumental in the building of the police barracks—still in use today—on Habersham Street.

Anderson died on February 8, 1888. The next day his body lay in Christ Church as throngs of Savannahians paid their last respects. On the day of his funeral, the entire police department, with the exception of a mounted squad, detailed for duty, formed in double ranks on Julian Street, facing the church.

From the church, Anderson's remains were given a military escort to Bonaventure Cemetery. Ahead of the procession was Anderson's riderless horse, led by an officer on foot, with the general's saber and boots strapped to the empty saddle.

Anderson's portrait, in a Confederate general's uniform, hangs in the police squad room at the barracks on Habersham Street.

In 1894, an impressive bronze bust showing the general in full military attire was unveiled at Anderson's gravesite in Bonaventure Cemetery.

William W. Gordon:
Young Man in a Hurry

At age forty-five, William Gordon suffered a heart attack and died; the man who had done so much in such a short period of time left a vacancy that was hard to fill. Yet, his premature death was not without warning. His wife had been chiding him for years for overwork and inattention to the family.

William was born in Augusta in 1796, the son of Ambrose Gordon, a wealthy landowner, Revolutionary War veteran, and contemporary of George Washington. The elder Gordon died when William was only eight and William was raised primarily by his mother. When he was seventeen, Gordon left for Rhode Island to finish school, and by the next year had received an appointment to the United States Military Academy, only the third Georgian to receive the honor.

In 1815, Gordon graduated and received an officer's commission, but resigned in less than a year to become an apprentice for James Moore Wayne, a Supreme Court Justice. It was through this association that he met his wife, Sarah Sites, Judge Moore's niece. William and Sarah were married on March 9, 1826.

Between 1834 and 1841, Gordon served several terms as an alderman and was Chatham County's representative in the Georgia Legislature for three sessions. He also served as state senator several terms.

But all this activity put a strain on Sarah, who had to care for their seven children, three of whom would die in childhood. In a letter to William dated December 8, 1839, she plainly states her case: "I do hope you will be home by Christmas at least. I cannot see what detains you. . . . I do hope you will not again be obliged to go to the legislature for I am sick and tired of it as I can well be."

On September 8, 1834, Gordon became Savannah's forty-fifth mayor, serving two and a half terms. He resigned to devote his time and energies to his growing passion, the railroad. William was the first president of the Central of Georgia Rail Road, and it is this endeavor that most Savannahians remember him for today.

A NEW INDUSTRY

Savannah had little use for a rail line during the first third of the 19th century until her fiercest competitor to the northeast, Charleston, developed a 90-mile track to Augusta. This took an economic toll on Savannah, and the city lost substantial export traffic. Soon, Savannah would try to catch up.

The city gave $500,000 to help establish a railroad line between Savannah and Macon. Within a few months, the state legislature, under Gordon's prodding, issued a charter for the rail line. Gordon assumed the then-unprecedented task of laying 160 miles of track from Savannah to the banks of the Ocmulgee River just south of Macon, at a cost of $10,000 per mile.

Activity was fervent but not without setbacks. Soon after the project started an economic depression threatened the line's existence, floods plagued the development of the track, and labor disputes came dangerously close to pushing the railroad into bankruptcy. In 1841, the company's stock dropped from $100 to $20 per share.

Gordon kept the project alive, but never saw its completion.

He died in 1842, only one year before the last rail was laid. The Central of Georgia became one of the most powerful institutions in Georgia and the entire South, holding its power well into the next century.

In 1850, the state legislature created Gordon County in his honor, and on June 25, 1882, there was unveiled in Wright Square an impressive marble monument in honor of William W. Gordon, man of commerce, young man in a hurry.

Dr. Francis Bland Tucker: Man of Faith and Devotion

Francis Bland Tucker stood in a white apron covered with blood. In the background boomed artillery. Serving in a wartime hospital in the first World War taught him valuable lessons that would remain with him for the balance of his life and help prepare him for a life of ministry. He would go home a different man.

NOBLE BEGINNINGS

Tucker was born in 1895, the twelfth and last child of Bishop Beverly Tucker and Anna Washington Tucker, both from Virginia. By all accounts, Tucker's family lineage is impressive. His mother had the distinction of being the last baby born in the ancestral home at Mount Vernon.

Henry George Tucker, a great-great-grandfather, served on Gen. George Washington's staff during the American Revolution and was present when Patrick Henry uttered those immortal words, "Give me liberty or give me death." It was Henry George Tucker who wrote down the words, saving them for posterity.

After graduating from the University of Virginia, Tucker sailed to Japan, where he taught English for two years under the watchful gaze of his brother Henry Tucker, missionary and president of St. Paul's college in Tokyo. Tucker returned to Virginia and enrolled in the Virginia Theological Seminary. But like many young men during that period, his studies were cut short by the war.

Tucker was part of the American Expeditionary Force that sailed to Europe in 1918 and eventually made its way to French battle-fields. Tucker, a private, worked in the operating room of an evac-uation hospital. Witnessing the horrors of war softened Tucker and gave him a pleasant demeanor, perfect for the ministry.

Returning home after the war, Tucker finished his theological studies and in 1920 was ordained as a priest in the Episcopal church.

Tucker's first parish was in Brunswick County, Virginia, where he served for six years. In 1926, he was named rector of St. John's in Washington, D.C., a position he held for sixteen years. While at St. John's, he was awarded a doctor of divinity degree and also developed a love for hymns. He authored six hymns, two of them original and four translated and paraphrased from Latin and Greek.

"Hymns are the best part of the service to me," Tucker wrote. Parishioners claim that he knew all of the 600 songs in the Episcopal hymnal by heart. His love for hymns took him a step fur-ther. He was chosen to serve on the joint commission on the revi-sion of the hymnal, a position he held from 1937-1946.

In 1945, at the age of fifty, Tucker became the rector of Christ Church, located on Johnson Square in Savannah. He became known as a gifted orator able to captivate a congregation. In fact, one of his parishioners stated that Dr. Tucker never read his ser-mons, unlike many ministers "now-a-days" who often read and preach by rote.

MIRACULOUS HEALING

In 1953, Dr. Tucker became ill and was sent to Emory University Hospital for testing. A series of x-rays showed a large tumor in his left lung. Not easily shaken, Dr. Tucker turned to what had brought him so far—prayer and faith. Not only did his con-gregation offer up prayers on his behalf, but they were joined by hundreds of friends and supporters.

An operation to remove the tumor was scheduled to take place within two weeks, but a post operative x-ray showed the impossi-ble: the tumor had shrunk 80 percent, and surgery was no longer necessary. His doctors called the breakthrough a "remarkable and drastic change." Dr. Tucker called it a miracle. "It is my firm conviction," he stated, "that the change was due to prayers and to God working through the doctors."

MINISTER OF PEACE

During the Civil Rights struggle of the 1960s, Dr. Tucker was a voice of reason among heated passions. He was often called to mediate disputes, urging reconciliation. In 1961, he headed a committee named by the Chatham County Commission to study the merits of being part of the Federal Food Stamp Program.

He also headed the board of the Family Service Agency, the forerunner of the Department of Family and Children Services (DFCAS). And he founded the Chatham County Conference, an interracial group of clergymen working toward the common goal of cooperation and peaceful change.

Dr. Tucker retired as rector of Christ Church in 1967 and was named the church's rector emeritus. He remained active, serving as a theological advisor to the commission that produced the 1979 revision of the Book of Common Prayer.

On New Year's Day 1984, at the age of eighty-nine, Dr. Tucker died. He could now utter those immortal words written by St. Paul nearly two thousand years before, "I have fought the good fight, I have finished my course. I have kept the faith."

Florence Martus,
Savannah's Waving Girl

Men returning home from sea would expect her, and men from foreign lands learned that she would always be there to greet them when they made port in Savannah. For forty-four years Florence Martus met every ship entering the Savannah River and every outgoing ship headed for the uncertainties of the Atlantic, becoming a seafaring legend.

Florence was born on Cockspur Island on August 8, 1868, in a frame building just north of Fort Pulaski. Her father, John Martus, a Civil War veteran, had recently completed forty years in the U.S. Army and was assigned as ordnance sergeant at the fort.

Until she was thirteen, Florence and her brother, George, led uneventful lives. But in 1881, a hurricane heading for Savannah blasted tiny Cockspur Island. Her family, fleeing harm's way, sought refuge in the nearby fort. But it, too, was threatened when water began to pour into the parade grounds. The Martus family finally found safety in one of the spiral stairwells deep within the fort.

During another colorful summer, Florence and George rescued the thirty-one crew members from a government dredge that had caught fire. All except one of the crew survived.

BY DAY AND BY NIGHT

When George accepted a job with the lighthouse service in 1887, Florence moved with him to the lighthouse keeper's house on Elba Island. It was from the cottage—a white, two-story house with a columned porch—that nineteen-year-old Florence began greeting ships. Waving a white handkerchief by day and a lantern by night, Florence welcomed both incoming ships and outgoing vessels.

She claimed to have waved at every vessel during her forty-four years on Elba Island. Years later, when asked in an interview by noted journalist Ernie Pyle if she ever missed a ship in all that time, she replied: "I was never too sick to get up when one was coming and I could always hear them coming."

FLORENCE MARTUS
1869 — 1943
SAVANNAH'S WAVING GIRL

Statue of Florence Martus on the east end of River Street on
the Savannah River. (Photo by Karri Cormican)

In time, Florence earned the nickname "The Waving Girl" and became known throughout the seafaring world, receiving letters from hundreds of sailors. Romantic stories emerged. The most popular story was that of a sailor sweetheart who was lost at sea. She waved at other seamen, the story goes, as a tribute to her lost love. Florence never verified the story, but she never denied it either.

A passenger on board a New York to Savannah steamer during the first quarter of the 20th century recalled Florence's greeting:

> The first I saw of her was at sunrise. The little white cottage where she lived was close to the bank. She was a little thing, thin but sturdy looking. The wind whipping at her skirt. . . almost tore the cloth out of her hand. The sun showed her hair as gray and curly with red color still in it. Her eyes were blue. She wasn't pretty but so alive. Her smile was one of the warmest I've ever seen. We saluted her with three blasts. I followed the ship's rail all the way to the stern, looking at her as long as she was visible.

After George retired from the lighthouse service in 1931, Florence, who never married, moved with him to an apartment at 642 E. Liberty Street. From Liberty Street she moved to Thunderbolt.

To celebrate her seventieth birthday, 3,000 people descended upon the parade grounds at Fort Pulaski. The U.S. Marine Corps Band and the Savannah Police Department Band played while the Coast Guard cutter *Tallapoose* fired a salute.

In November 1943, a Liberty ship, the *SS Florence Martus,* slipped smoothly down the ways after a champagne christening. She was the thirteenth of eighty-eight liberty ships built during World War II in Savannah.

A TRIBUTE

On the banks of the Savannah River, at the east end of River Street, a 17-foot statue was erected in Florence's memory. The statue of a young woman, with a collie at her side, waves a handkerchief and continues to welcome seaman from around the world.

The Day Babe Ruth
Played in Savannah

Babe Ruth lumbered out of the dugout, noticeably slower and heavier. Every eye in the stadium was on him. He tapped the end of the bat against his cleats and stepped up to the plate.

The pitcher, just a college kid, stared eagerly at his catcher. He'd never faced such a legend before and probably never would again. If he could strike Ruth out, he'd have the story of a lifetime.

The pitcher began his windup and released the ball. Ruth waited patiently, bringing his big bat around. The crack of ball against wood echoed throughout the stadium as a line drive shot past the first-base line, just high enough to clear the rightfield fence. As it landed in the grass between the concrete bleachers and wooden seats, small boys scrambled for the priceless souvenir.

Ruth began his slow triumphant march around the bases as fans went wild. They had gotten what they came for, a home run from the Sultan of Swat. Yet this wasn't Yankee Stadium or the Polo Grounds, but Savannah Municipal Stadium—April 4, 1935.

On February 26 of the same year the baseball world was turned upside down. Ruth, after nearly two decades of dominance with the New York Yankees, was traded to the Boston Braves. Signing a three-year contract, he would see action as a player, assistant manager, and team vice president for $25,000 per year. This was an impressive salary during the throes of the Great Depression, but it was only a fraction of the earnings that Ruth had once commanded. As far back as 1920 he had signed with the Yankees for an unprecedented $125,000 a year. By all accounts Ruth's career was drawing to a close.

Despite this, the forty-year-old, 215-pound slugger could still pack a stadium. And the Braves, needing a financial boost, were banking on that for the 1935 season.

Arriving in Boston to join the Braves in March, Ruth was greeted by the city's mayor, the Massachusetts lieutenant governor, dignitaries, and several thousand fans. After the festivities, he boarded a Florida-bound train for yet another spring training.

"In some respects it's still like a dream to me," Ruth told reporters.

"I can't realize that I won't trot out into Yankee Stadium for the opening game next month. But I'm tickled to death with the switch."

Spring training became excruciating for the rotund slugger who never cared for conditioning and was known for his opulent lifestyle. But hard work and determination finally paid off and by the end of spring training some of the magic was back in his swing.

"SAVANNAH TO GET BIG LEAGUE NINES. BABE RUTH TO BE SEEN IN ACTION," read the March 21 headline of the *Savannah Morning News*. As soon as the news broke, Municipal Stadium groundskeepers began putting clay along the base lines and pitcher's mound. Coats of paint were added and bunting prepared. After about a week the diamond was ready for the big leaguers.

Built in 1927, Municipal Stadium, the predecessor of Grayson, became a local favorite. High school football games and pro and semi-pro baseball games were held there, as were political rallies and even a visit from President Franklin Delano Roosevelt in 1933.

The stadium was destroyed, however, when a hurricane slammed into Savannah in 1940. All that remains of the original stadium are the concrete outfield bleachers and the diamond. The present brick-and-concrete grandstand behind home plate was built in 1941, and the park was rededicated as Grayson Stadium.

An exhibition game was set between the Braves and South Georgia Teachers College (later renamed Georgia Southern). Despite the obvious fact that South Georgia had little chance of winning, few seemed to care. Just catching a glimpse of Ruth in action justified missing work, skipping school, or shirking household duties. Grandstand tickets cost a dollar, too rich for many in those days. Most opted for the bleachers at fifty cents a ticket. Students were admitted for a quarter.

The Braves' train arrived in Savannah around 11 a.m. and was met by a large crowd. As the slugger stepped off the Atlantic Coast Line train, he was swarmed by reporters. From the train station Ruth made his way by cab to the DeSoto Hotel on Liberty Street. Giving instructions to the hotel clerk to keep his suite number a secret, Ruth rushed to his room.

But soon the secret was out. Reporters and fans began knocking on his door. True to form, Ruth, good humored, gave brief interviews.

He showed particular kindness to the children, remembering his own childhood days growing up in a Baltimore industrial school for boys.

How many homers are you going to hit this year, asked a reporter. "I dunno," said Ruth. "It's according to how things go. Sometimes you can knock the ears off the ball. Other times things don't go right, but I'm going to do my best.

"You know," he added, "I'm not as young as I used to be. I feel it, too."

The next day the Braves faced South Georgia on the playing field. Unruly crowds at the stadium, trying to slip into the Braves' dugout, had to be kept at bay by a police barricade. But a few cunning boys rushed the line and made it through to shake hands with the obliging legend.

The Braves owned the day, pounding the college, 15-1. The Teachers hit safely only six times, two of which came from a Braves catcher loaned to them for the day. Ruth went to bat three times.

In his first plate appearance, Ruth reached base on an infield error. In his second at bat, he hit his home run. In the fifth, he swung at a pitch so hard that he almost fell down. On the next pitch, he grounded out to the second baseman.

Leaving the stadium in the sixth inning, Ruth was trailed by a ragtag group of kids. A dozen boys clinging to his car had to be pried off before he could drive away.

Back at the hotel, Ruth met more fans, signed more autographs, and spoke to more reporters. One would imagine that he would have been happy to leave Savannah, but he was headed to Fayetteville, North Carolina, for another exhibition game and another first-class mauling by adoring fans.

This was Ruth's last year in the majors. After 22 years, 714 home runs, and a .342 lifetime batting average, he finally hung up his cleats. Age, hard living, and poor health had done what no fastball could ever do. In 1948, he would die of throat cancer. It would be seventeen years before another homerun king, a skinny eighteen-year-old minor leaguer named Henry Aaron, would play on the same diamond, adding another chapter to Savannah's rich baseball history.

Gen. Lafayette McLaws:
Merely a Bust in Forsyth Park?

Taking my small nephew for a walk through Forsyth Park, we happened upon the Confederate Memorial, flanked on the north side by the bust of Francis Bartow and on the south side by a bust of Gen. Lafayette McLaws. After a myriad of questions, I tried my best to make my answers suit both the imagination and the inquisitiveness of a small boy.

The soldier on top of the monument, I told him, represented all of the men and boys who fought for the South long ago. The two men on the sides were brave and noble officers who led gallant charges in battle and finally succumbed to overwhelming odds.

"But who did they fight?" he asked.

"Americans."

"Who were they?" he pressed further.

Again I replied, "Americans."

The confused look on his face told me that he couldn't quite grasp the fact that Americans would fight other Americans. So I turned his attention to the two busts at the base of the great monument.

One is Francis Bartow, a native Savannahian, I told him, who was killed in the first major battle of the war—Bull Run, or what many Southerners call First Manassas. The other, Gen. Lafayette McLaws, a native Georgian, survived the war, proving to be a brave soldier. Satisfied with these answers (at least for the time being), he turned his attention to more pressing matters, namely pigeons and squirrels.

Maj. Gen. Lafayette McLaws was, indeed, a brave man and warrior in every sense of the word. Born in Augusta, Georgia, on January 15, 1821, he spent a year studying at the University of Virginia before transferring to West Point, where he graduated in 1842. Like many cadets during that era, McLaws befriended several young officers, some who would prove to be allies in the upcoming Civil War and some who would be deadly foes. One such friend was a young cadet by the name of Ulysses S. "Sam" Grant.

Bust of Gen. Lafayette McLaws, with Confederate monument in the background, located in Forsyth Park. (Photo by Karri Cormican)

A story was told by the late Virginia Pritchard, McLaws' great-granddaughter, of her ancestor's friendship with Grant at West Point. According to Mrs. Pritchard, when the future president was absent at roll call, his friend McLaws covered for him by answering when his name was called. "Thankfully, the two never met in battle," Mrs. Pritchard added.

After graduation, McLaws spent four years in Pensacola and in what was then called Indian Territory—until the outbreak of the Mexican War.

BAPTISM OF FIRE

Joining the American occupation force at Corpus Christi, Lieutenant McLaws longed to taste battle. Soon, his wish would come true. He was reassigned to Monterrey, Mexico, where the Mexican Army put up some of the fiercest fighting of the war and American casualties ran high. After Monterrey, McLaws joined Gen. Winfield Scott and took part in the siege of Vera Cruz.

The friendships and acquaintances McLaws made during the war were impressive: Capt. Robert E. Lee, A.P. Hill, Thomas "Stonewall" Jackson, Joseph Johnston, George Stoneman, George Pickett, John B. Magruder, and George McClellan. After the end of hostilities in Mexico, McLaws served in New Mexico and also took part in the controversial Mormon War in Utah.

FIGHTING IN VIRGINIA

On January 19, 1861, Georgia passed an ordinance of secession and by March McLaws had resigned his officer's commission and returned to Georgia. In less than a month he was a newly commissioned major in the Confederate States Army.

Rising to the rank of major general, McLaws participated in all of the Virginia and Maryland campaigns as part of the Army of Northern Virginia and personally commanded a division at Gettysburg, earning a reputation as a stubborn defensive fighter. McLaws' military career continued to rise, only to be blemished by a controversy with his commanding officer, former West Point classmate and fellow Augusta native Gen. James Longstreet.

After the Confederate failure at Knoxville, Longstreet leveled charges against McLaws, accusing him of failure to execute orders and a general lack of cooperation. Many believed Longstreet needed a scapegoat for a poorly executed campaign, but a military court found McLaws guilty on several charges and he was relieved of command.

Only through President Jefferson Davis' intervention did McLaws obtain another commission. He was placed in control of Confederate forces in the District of Georgia and was also responsible for Savannah's defenses. It proved a fruitless cause. In a few months, Sherman and his troops burst through the state and McLaws and the entire Confederate army in the area had little choice but to flee harm's way.

After the war, McLaws opened an insurance business. In 1876, President Grant, McLaws' old friend and former Mexican War comrade in arms, appointed McLaws to the position of collector of the Internal Revenue Service in Savannah and later postmaster of Savannah. He was active in Confederate veterans' organizations for many years after the war and wrote several articles on his unit's part in battle.

McLaws died unexpectedly at his Anderson Street home in Savannah on July 24, 1897. He is buried in Laurel Grove Cemetery and his bust rests in a place of honor in the middle of Forsyth Park for a new generation to ponder.

John Houstoun:
The Signer Who Did Not Sign

Imagine passing up the opportunity of a lifetime. What about of a generation? Or of a nation's history? That's exactly what happened to Savannahian John Houstoun, would-be signer of the Declaration of Independence.

Houstoun, at twenty-six, was one of the most influential Georgia delegates sent to the Continental Congress in Philadelphia. Having studied law in South Carolina and having traveled through the colonies, Houstoun had already rubbed shoulders with Ben Franklin, Thomas Jefferson, and John Adams. He supported the call for public meetings to protest Parliament's closing of Boston's harbor and was soon referred to as a hot-headed rebel.

Along with Noble W. Jones, Archibald Bulloch, and George Walton, Houstoun issued the public call for a meeting at Tondee's Tavern on July 27, 1774, for citizens to discuss their rights as American subjects.

In 1775, passions flared and the colonies, torn between loyalty to their king and the desire for independence, prepared for war. The delegates of the Continental Congress were no different; they were split between loyalists and what many called traitors—later called patriots.

When a Declaration of Independence was proposed, pandemonium erupted among the delegates. Dr. John Zubly of Georgia, minister of the Independent Presbyterian Church in Savannah and ardent supporter of the crown, remarked, "A Republican Government is no better than a government of devils." It is with this sentiment that he embarked on a journey to inform Royal Governor Wright of the delegation's alleged treason.

MISSED OPPORTUNITY

Hot on his heels was young Houstoun, the youngest and best fit of the distinguished but aged delegates. He intercepted Zubly, but in doing so missed the opportunity to attach his name to the history-altering document. Therefore Georgia has three, instead of four, signers: Button Gwinnett, Lyman Hall, and George Walton. Yet, this story is not without controversy, and some historians claim that it cannot be fully substantiated.

Another theory, less dramatic, and also based on conjecture, places Houstoun in Savannah during the signing. He had been called back to Georgia to counteract the influence of Zubly, also in Georgia at the time.

Whichever theory is true, the simple fact remains: John Houstoun, slated to sign the Declaration of Independence, was absent and missed his opportunity to add his signature to the document that set the world on end.

Houstoun's list of accomplishments and service to his country, state, and city are impressive, yet he was also beset by controversy. During the first part of the Revolutionary War, he served as Georgia's governor and was responsible for mobilizing the state's militia. Houstoun again served as Georgia's governor from 1784-1785.

Early in his first term as governor, Houstoun led a military expedition against the British in St. Augustine. Houstoun, however, without military experience and training, ran into problems. His offensive got no further than the Georgia-Florida state line, not so much because of military weakness, but because of internal dissension.

In 1790, Houstoun became Savannah's first mayor, serving a one-year term. During his short administration Savannah continued its expansion. Lots were laid out, as well as wards, parks, and squares. The first act of the Houstoun administration was to appoint a treasurer, clerk, constable, and clerk of the market. When the city council presented the city's first budget on May 18, 1790, it totaled 1,250 pounds.

In 1792, Houstoun was elected Judge of the Eastern Judicial Circuit. On July 20, 1796, exactly twenty years after the birth of his beloved nation, Houstoun died at his White Bluff home, just outside of Savannah.

The distinguished patriot, former governor, mayor, lawyer, and judge lies in an unmarked grave in an unknown location. In 1821, Houston County in Georgia was named in his honor. Houston Street in Savannah was also named for him. His portrait hangs in the Savannah City Hall rotunda.

The fabric of early Georgia's economic, political, and civic life were greatly impacted, even altered, by the efforts and devotion of John Houstoun of Savannah, the signer who did not sign.

Juliette Gordon Low:
Girl Scouts Founder, Little Rebel

Nicknamed Daisy by her family and friends, Juliette Gordon Low's life spanned the years between the end of the antebellum south and the two world wars. Her life's work was the formation of the Girl Scouts of the United States of America, and her birthplace on Oglethorpe Avenue has become a National Historic Landmark that serves as a pilgrimage for thousands of Girl Scouts each year.

Born on Halloween in 1860 to William Washington Gordon II and Eleanor McKenzie Gordon, Juliette was described as a sensitive and attentive girl who enjoyed a happy childhood. She attended private school in Virginia and later a French school in New York, where she developed a lifelong appreciation of the arts. She wrote poetry, acted in plays, and later painted and became a sculptress.

MEETING GENERAL SHERMAN

As a small child, Juliette remembered the capture of Savannah by Union troops. Gen. William Tecumseh Sherman, who knew Juliette's mother before the war, paid a visit to Mrs. Gordon when he was in Savannah. Juliette noticed one of Sherman's aides with an empty sleeve. The officer said, "Little girl, don't you feel sorry for me?" She remarked: "I shouldn't wonder if my papa did it. He shoots lots of Yankees!" After a moment of tense silence, the general broke into laughter.

Mrs. Gordon and her three children were given passage to her parents' home in Chicago to wait for the end of the war. When news came of the Confederate surrender, Chicago's streets erupted in celebration. Juliette, ever the little Rebel, perched herself on a gate post and sang "Dixie."

Though Juliette was reared during Reconstruction, she still led a privileged life. On December 21, 1886, at Christ Episcopal Church in Savannah, she married William Mackay Low, a wealthy Englishman. Soon, the couple moved to England, where Juliette enjoyed an active social life and the splendor of the Victorian age. Juliette wasn't bound by the rigidness of the era and was often considered a maverick.

Juliette Gordon Low at a young age. (Photo courtesy Juliette Gordon Low Girl Scout National Center)

Once, apparently bored at a social outing, she left wearing a formal evening gown to go trout fishing with author Rudyard Kipling.

During the Spanish-American War, Juliette returned to the United States, and with her mother's help established a convalescent hospital for soldiers in Florida. Her father, a former Confederate captain, was stationed there as a general in the U.S. Army.

After her husband died in 1905, Juliette regretted not having any children of her own. By this time, she also experienced a decline in health due to a series of ear infections, which eventually led to complete and permanent deafness. This crucible would prove to be the turning point in her life.

In 1911, at age fifty, Juliette met recently retired British army officer Sir Robert Baden-Powell, who had recently established the Boy Scouts. Inspired by his ideas, she wrote: "A sort of intuition comes over me . . . that I might make more out of my life and that he has ideas, which if I follow them, will open a more useful sphere of work before me in the future."

Juliette returned to the United States and immediately went to work. Enthused, she telephoned her cousin, Nina Pape, and said, "Come right over! I've got something for all the girls of Savannah and all America, and all the world, and we're going to start it tonight.' Three months later, on March 12, 1912, Daisy Gordon, Juliette's niece, was registered as the first member of the Girl Scouts.

Juliette traveled extensively to develop the Girl Scouts, making speeches, organizing troops, choosing leaders, and writing handbooks, all the while bearing the expenses herself. In 1914, she sold her beloved string of pearls to help defray costs.

By 1916, over 5,000 girls were enrolled in the Girl Scouts. Juliette then turned her energies to establishing scouting worldwide and arranged the first World Wide Committee of Girl Scouts. In 1926, the World Conference of Girl Scouts was held; twenty-six nations were represented.

Juliette died from cancer on January 27, 1927, and was buried in her Girl Scout uniform in Laurel Grove Cemetery in Savannah.

JULIETTE'S INFLUENCE GROWS

In 1948, President Harry Truman signed a bill authorizing a

stamp in Juliette's honor. During World War II, a Liberty ship was named for her. In 1954, the city named a new elementary school after her and on December 2, 1986, President Ronald Reagan signed a bill naming the new federal building in Savannah the Juliette Low Building. A bronze bust of Juliette was authorized to be placed in the Georgia Hall of Fame in the capitol rotunda in Atlanta.

From eighteen members in 1912, the Girl Scouts has grown to an organization with over three million members and has become part of the fabric of American life.

Henry McAlpin:
Empire Building on the Backs of Others

Few can dispute the fact that Henry McAlpin created an impressive empire that helped build Savannah. Yet, how he created his empire would not pass today's standards of morality or human rights.

Born in Scotland in 1777, Henry McAlpin immigrated to the United States in 1804 at the age of twenty-seven. Arriving at the port of Charleston, South Carolina, McAlpin made his way to Savannah by 1812. He was described at the time as a man of ruddy countenance with straightforward blue eyes and a strong chin.

McAlpin married Helen McGinnis, a native Charlestonian. Together they had eight children, but only seven survived. When Helen died prematurely at the age of thirty-one, the children were separated. The boys remained with their father in Savannah but the girls were sent to Charleston to live with relatives.

Ambitious to establish himself as a businessman, McAlpin acquired property before he became naturalized. McAlpin's friend William I. Scott purchased the Hermitage Plantation for him at a public auction on April 4, 1815. The Hermitage, located on the banks of the Savannah River, was one of several area plantations known as the Savannah River Plantations.

SAVANNAH GREY BRICK

In 1819, McAlpin constructed a brick manufacturing plant at the Hermitage. The Hermitage became the only plantation in the area to earn the bulk of its revenue from non-agricultural production.

Savannah, in need of building supplies after a devastating fire in 1820, turned to McAlpin for help. The brick plant became a thriving business, supplying thousands of bricks to help rebuild the city.

Much of the brick produced became known as "Savannah Grey Brick." Made from gray clay found on the plantation, the brick—which is actually a reddish brown color—was popular because of its low cost of production and its subsequent low selling price.

The Central of Georgia Railroad building was built with Savannah Grey Brick, as was Fort Pulaski. Many of the older homes still standing in Savannah are built with Savannah Grey Brick. This inexpensive brick, once sold at cut-rate prices, now demands a premium.

It was McAlpin's brick manufacturing that created the need for a railway, the first in the United States. In 1820, he needed to move a building from one kiln to another, so he constructed a crude rail system. A car pulled by a horse ran on track connecting the two kilns. After its use, it was disassembled.

Not only did McAlpin run a thriving brick business, but he also owned a foundry and lumber mill. In addition, he owned rice fields on the low-lying areas of his plantation. Of course, to have such an enterprise takes considerable manpower and McAlpin fueled his industry on the backs of slaves.

Not only was the slave trade lucrative for McAlpin, but he also utilized it to the utmost. He used his slaves as a means to maintain a positive cash flow. He bought, borrowed, and traded using slaves. On several occasions, he secured loans using slaves as collateral.

Yet, by every account examined he wasn't a harsh master, at least by 19th century standards. He would allow older slaves, no longer able to work, to remain on the plantation, and he usually kept slave families intact, which was rare in the slave business.

At the time of his death in 1851, McAlpin owned 172 field slaves valued at $53,490 and 16 house slaves valued at $4,800. McAlpin was buried in a cemetery on the Hermitage Plantation, but was later reburied at the Colonial Cemetery in Savannah.